Dear  Children

THE MESSAGES OF
OUR LADY OF MEDJUGORJE

THEMATICALLY PRESENTED WITH PICTURES
BY
DR. KELLY BOWRING AND VINCENT MURRAY

✝ ✝ ✝

"Dear children!
I ask you to accept and to live these messages...
each day read the messages
that I have given you
and transform them into life.
Thank you for having responded to my call."
- OUR LADY OF MEDJUGORJE -

✝ ✝ ✝

Two Hearts Press, LLC
www.TwoHeartsPress.com

Text Graphic Design: Kim Litzelman
Book Cover Design: Bonaventure Web Design

Library of Congress Control Number: 2013930816

Published by Two Hearts Press, LLC, Cumming, GA, USA
Printed in the United States of America

ISBN-13: 978-0-9802292-3-3
ISBN-10: 0-9802292-3-5

To order copies of this book:
Please call toll-free (24/7)
1-800-BookLog (266-5564)

Or fax orders to:
1-419-281-6883

Or order **book or e-book** on our website at:
www.TwoHeartsPress.com

TABLE OF CONTENTS

BOOK ENDORSEMENTS

M edjugorje has a special place in my heart, since it was there I made the decision to give my life to Christ as a priest. The alleged apparitions of Our Lady in Medjugorje are truly a gift for our time because they are calling us to deeper relationship and walk with Christ. They call us to make use of the sacraments in which God is truly present. While we await the church to officially respond to these events that are taking place in Medjugorje, Bowring and Murray have provided a tremendous resource for us in categorizing Our Lady's alleged messages according to over 140 topical themes. This book serves as a valuable tool to help us more easily absorb the messages, which she is giving to us.

Fr. Charles Mangano
Pastor of Cure' of Ars Church, Merrick, NY

B owring and Murray have devotedly accomplished what many followers of Medjugorje have desired for many years. For those of us that have a strong devotion to Our Blessed Mother and for those that wish to understand Our Holy Mother's Messages in a perceptible format of category, this book is indispensable. I have been a devotee of Medjugorje for over twenty years and to date have taken pilgrimages to Medjugorje and I have participated in the publication of almost 200 "Our Mother Queen of Peace Newsletters." I have read many books about Medjugorje and they are all good, but this one is unique. It is a study manual for those who wish to be perfect spiritually.

Fino Giordano
Coordinator of Our Blessed Mother Queen of Peace, Long Island, NY

With great devotion and as a labor of love, Bowring and Murray have given us this beautiful gift of coordinating Our Lady's messages from Medjugorje in a unique fashion. They have diligently prepared this work to give us specific categories, which we might want to read more about or study at any particular time in our lives. They also make it so easy for us to use their book as a source of reference in order to share Our Lady's messages with others.

We feel truly blessed to be in Our Lady's army with such devoted prayer warriors.

Penny Abbruzzese
Publisher of "Mary's Mantle," Long Island, NY

"THIS BOOK IS AN EXCELLENT SOURCE

TO HELP LIVE AND SHARE

OUR LADY'S MESSAGES."

- Wayne Weible

ACKNOWLEDGEMENTS

We would like to express our gratitude and thanksgiving to God for His Grace and His Inspiration to undertake and persevere in this effort and to assist Our Lady of Medjugorje in fulfilling His Plan for the salvation of all mankind. We would also like to express our thanksgiving to God for the gift of His Mother, in this our time, and the special graces He offers to all of us through His Mother during this time of His Mercy.

We offer a heart-felt thanks to you, Mary Most Holy, the Queen of Peace, for selecting us to assist you in your mission. You have invited all of us to become missionaries of your message and to share them with the whole world.

We have undertaken this work as a humble service to the Mother of God, having full confidence in her power of intercession before God that this effort will bear much fruit according to God's Will.

A special thank you goes to Kelvin Hui, who spent months of his time arranging these messages by subject within chapter, to Aili Hsin, for her untiring effort to help in typing, to Terence Fu, Andrew Ko and Calvin Hung for offering their computer skills, to Mary Sue Eck of *Medjugorje Magazine*, Larry Landolphi and Joseph Mixan who provided the pictures, and to Penny Abbruzzese and Fino Giordano for their encouragement.

We ask Our Lady of Medjugorje to bless all of you with Her Motherly Blessing. May God Bless us all and bring us to life everlasting.   Amen.

PREFACE

"I AM THE QUEEN OF PEACE.
I HAVE COME TO TELL THE WORLD
THAT GOD EXISTS."

First words spoken by
Our Heavenly Mother in Medjugorje (June 25, 1981)

ଔ

Like many people throughout the world, we believe we have been called to assist Our Lady of Medjugorje, to help fulfill God's purpose in sending her into our world over the past 31+ years. We believe His purpose in sending Our Lady from Heaven to give us messages for our times is for the salvation of all mankind.

Our Lady of Medjugorje is the author of this work and we are just her servants responding to her call, collaborating together to organize her messages in way that is easier for the reader to assimilate.

We believe this book will serve as an instructional and meditative resource, to be used by clergy, the faithful and all people of good will, to teach not only Catholics and Christians, but the entire world, what Our Lady of Medjugorje has been revealing in her messages since she first started appearing in June of 1981.

Our Lady indicates that she wants us to pray so as to understand why she is coming. She says, *"If you pray, God will help you to discover the true reason for my coming."*

Mary is giving us messages from Heaven, messages from God. She is calling us to seek and do His Will. God's Will is for us to become perfect, as He is Perfect and to become holy, as He is Holy. That means for us to love Him in this world and to be with Him in the next. With our free will, we can choose to ignore God; to disobey God's Commandments and keep on committing serious sin; to not pray or include God in our lives; to not listen to His Mother as she tries to teach us what we must do for our own salvation and the salvation of others.

The reality that God is sending Jesus' Mother, Mary, to give us messages from Heaven in our times is a great gift to behold. What a time we live in! Now is the time of God's Mercy! Never in the history of Marian apparitions has Jesus sent His Mother for such a prolonged period of time and with so many messages. She says, "*These are special times,*" "*These are my times,*" and she says that these are her last appearances here on earth in this form.   The time remaining is short for us to respond to her call.

Although we can speculate when we think Our Lady's appearances will end, no one really knows the time. What we do know is that Our Lady has said: "*These times are times of special grace from God*"; and that we should be thankful to God for each day that He allows her to be with us. Our Lady has given us a hint of how much longer these events will continue. In the recent message to Mirjana, she said:

> *My coming to you, my children, is God's Love. God is sending me to warn you and to show you the right way. Do not shut your eyes before the truth, my children. **Your time is a short time**. Do not permit delusions to begin ruling over you. The way on which I desire to lead you is the way of peace and love. This is the way which leads to my Son, your God. Give me your hearts that I may put my Son in them and make my apostles of you – **apostles of peace and love**.*

Only God knows when these appearances by Our Lady of Medjugorje will end. All things will be in God's time. Now is our time! We all have a choice to make! Mary is pleading for us to make God the center of our lives; to eliminate all sin; to take seriously what she is saying in her messages, and to put her messages into practice in our lives. If we do not listen and act on her words, we will surely deserve what is coming. When the apparitions end in Medjugorje, and when this period of God's Mercy ends, then God will bring His justice. Then it will be too late for many in this world. As you read and study Mary's messages, you will also realize, that **your prayer** to God, **is the central most important part of her messages.**

The question is what kind of prayer, how often, and how much is enough. It is a daily practice for the six visionaries of Medjugorje to spend at least 4 hours each day in prayer: attending daily Mass; praying the mysteries of the Rosary, and praying with their families in morning and evening prayer.

Mary says, *"Pray without cease."* Many times she has emphasized in her messages the need for prayer by just saying, ***"Pray! Pray! Pray!"***

The visionaries have been shown by Mary why so much prayer is required. Mary is here in our time to save as many souls as possible. **She needs our prayer to accomplish God's plan**, for the salvation of all mankind.

The visionaries have also seen the secrets, which are events that will happen in their future. Our prayer can help to lessen the severity of some of these events, which will affect many people and change the world we live in. If we do not act now and heed our Mother's call for help, then we will regret this very much when the secrets start to unfold.

Our Lady told the visionary Mirjana the following:

> *Mirjana, I chose you, and I told you everything that is necessary. I entrusted you with the knowledge of many abominations, which you must carry with dignity. Think of me, and how much I too shed tears because of this. You must **always be brave**. You quickly understood my messages, and so you must understand that now I must leave. **Be brave...!***

Entrusting to her the tenth secret, Our Lady told her that for the rest of her life she would have one apparition on March 18 of each year.

We in the West have become desensitized to violence and horror, by what is presented in the movies, on TV and the disasters that we witness happening in other parts of the world. As long as we are not affected by the horror and terror, the general thinking is, so what, life goes on. We believe that the secret events that are coming will change this way of thinking and will make us ponder God's presence and His power in our world. The first few secrets may be limited to a city, country or area of the world, but the visionaries say that the final secrets will affect the whole world.

So the question is, do we listen to Mary and start praying more now, or do we wait to see if this is all real, and hope, as the first secret is played out, that it does not affect us or those we love.   On the contrary, Mary has said, *"Don't wait for the secrets,* **live my messages now.** *"*

She also said, *"God gives me this time as a gift to you so that I may instruct and lead you on the path of salvation. Dear children, now you do not comprehend this grace, but soon* **a time will come when you will lament for these messages.** *"*

All of the messages in this book are Mary's exact words. We have not offered any commentary or explanations beyond the introduction. Her words are clear and easy to understand. We have taken these messages and arranged them by subject in chapters and then chronologically within each chapter. We hope this will make it easier for everyone to learn and put into practice what she is teaching us. We hope these messages will fulfill God's purpose of bringing you **closer to Jesus** and to the life of love and peace God wants you to have. So much so, **Jesus sent His own Mother to be your guide** and instructor and to give you hundreds of heavenly messages by which to live your life by! How will you respond to her heavenly call?

INTRODUCTION

"GOD HAS CHOSEN EACH ONE OF YOU

IN ORDER TO USE YOU

FOR THE GREAT PLAN

OF THE SALVATION OF MANKIND."

Our Lady of Medjugorje

℅

Jesus' Mother, the Queen of Peace, is coming to earth today, sent by God from Heaven, with an urgent message for the whole world.

The Blessed Virgin Mary, has been reportedly visiting and speaking to six children – **Vicka** Ivankovic-Mijatovic, **Ivan** Dragicevic, **Mirjana** Dragicevic-Soldo, **Ivanka** Ivankovic-Elez, **Jakov** Colo, and **Marija** Pavlovic-Lunetti – since June 24, 1981. It has been over 31+ years that she has been appearing to these children (visionaries) in a small village called Medjugorje, located in the country of Bosnia Herzegovina, within the former country of Yugoslavia.

In that time, **over 40 million pilgrims** have visited Medjugorje, including 300,000 religious, priests, and bishops. Over **500 healings** have been medically documented in Medjugorje since the apparitions began; and over **500 men** have stated that their vocation to become a priest was due to Medjugorje. Millions of pilgrims have also reported witnessing and experiencing miraculous signs and wonders — like the sun dancing in the sky, rosaries turning "gold", and so many types of spiritual healings.

Its no wonder then that Bl. John Paul II stated personally that Medjugorje is the spiritual heart of the world today and its hope!

The visionaries, four women and two men, to whom Our Lady of Medjugorje has been revealing her messages for the world, are now adults. They are married and have families. She has stated that these appearances will be the last time God will allow her to appear in our world in this way.

Mary is giving instructions and heavenly messages to these visionaries for them to share with the whole world. God wants to give you an important divine message from Heaven. He is sending His Mother today to give it to you. This book is our effort to reveal to you what she is saying.

God is telling us that we must listen to her urgent words and return to a path leading to Him before it is too late. Three things are being requested of us. Our Lady is asking us to read, live, and spread these heavenly messages. This book is the tool to use to respond to these heavenly requests.

This book provides all the messages to date of Our Lady of Medjugorje, and presents them not in just chronological or random order, but thematically by topic so that you can read what Heaven is saying about various specific themes, all in one place.

As you read each page, **you will find yourself returning to this guidebook daily as your source to understanding, living, and spreading joyfully the heavenly messages of Our Lady** given to us in these times!

Famous Supporters

There have been many significant supporters of this still-ongoing apparition.

Blessed John Paul II wrote in his own hand, *"I thank Sophia (a friend) for everything concerning Medjugorje. I, too, go there everyday as a pilgrim in my prayers."* He also said: *"Medjugorje is the hope for the entire world, the spiritual heart of the world."*

Blessed Mother Teresa, again in her own hand, wrote: *"We are all praying one Hail Mary before Holy Mass to Our Lady of Medjugorje!"*

Hundreds of cardinals and bishops have visited Medjugorje as pilgrims (or have expressed their support for what is happening there), along with tens of thousands of priests and tens of millions of lay pilgrims.

Medjugorje and the Church

The alleged apparitions of the Blessed Mother in Medjugorje reportedly continue daily, and the Catholic Church has continued to investigate these events during the past 31+ years. The fruits of Medjugorje are very good! Because of Medjugorje, millions of people are praying, fasting, and attending Holy Mass. And many people are now praying the daily Rosary with their families and going to confession regularly.

Pope Benedict XVI had recently appointed a new Vatican Commission, which was given the responsibility to investigate the Medjugorje events in order to determine if they are authentic and deserving of more official recognition or simply to continue without being unauthenticated. The six visionaries have been interviewed by the Vatican Commission to testify regarding their visions and conversations with the Mother of God. To date, the Vatican says private pilgrimages are permitted to Medjugorje and that the reported heavenly messages may be read and shared.

As we await the Church's updated decision regarding these events, **let us prayerfully respond to her call now**, which is to renounce sin and to live the Gospel message more faithfully.

In the meantime, we are reminded that no Church recognition or imprimatur is necessary for the reading, publication, and spreading of private revelations, prophecies, or miracles (so long as they have not been condemned). With this in mind, we wish to move forward with the heart and mind of the Church and thus with her blessing.

It is important to note again that it is not against the Church or her canon law to read and meditate on reliable apparitions and their messages, even on the ones that have not been officially fully approved by the Church, provided they have not been condemned and do not in any way disagree with doctrine and Church teaching. The authors recognize and gladly accept that the final authority regarding the supernatural character of the apparitions, locutions, and heavenly messages in this book rests always and finally with the Magisterium of the Catholic Church.

Pope Urban VIII also gave sound advice about following reported, reliable heavenly apparitions, saying:

> *In cases like this, it is **better to believe** than not to believe, for, if you believe, and it is proven true, you will be happy that you have believed, because Our Holy Mother asked it. If you believe, and it should be proven false, you will receive all blessings as if it had been true, because you believed it to be true.*

The Ten Secrets

Mary is reportedly giving the visionaries **ten secrets** of worldwide significance. The first three secrets of Medjugorje have to do with warnings. According to visionary, Mirjana, *"**The first two secrets** come as advance **warnings** for the whole world and as proof the Blessed Virgin Mary is here in Medjugorje,"* while **the third secret concerns a** *"permanent, indestructible and beautiful"* **Sign** that will appear in Medjugorje on the hill of the first apparitions, which will remain until the end of time.

Our Lady has promised to leave **a supernatural, indestructible, and visible sign** on the mountain where she first appeared. Our Lady said:

> *This sign will be given for the atheists. You faithful already have signs and you have become the sign for the atheists. You faithful must not wait for the sign before you convert; convert soon. This time is a time of grace for you. You can never thank God enough for His grace. The time is for deepening your faith and for your conversion.* **When the sign comes, it will be too late for many.**

The sign is to bring many to reconciliation and conversion. The Sign that will appear in Medjugorje will bring great joy to many. But, pertaining to this Sign, Mirjana said: *"After the visible Sign those who are alive will have little time for conversion."* It seems that many will see the miracle and believe – there will be many conversions – but that others may at this point see the miracle and still not believe or convert. Mary speaks to us today, saying: *"***Hurry to be converted. I need your prayers and your penance.***"* In this regard, she also said: *"Return to prayer! Nothing is more needed than prayer."*

The final seven secrets are very serious. Visionary Mirjana says that Mary asks us to prepare spiritually and not to panic, but to convert now. Mirjana says that God is love, only love, and that cruelty and evil come from Satan. Those who freely choose Satan and disobey God's Commandments will perish. If there are divine punishments, they come for the sins of the world and are always reparative. God is a father who lovingly chastises His children whom He loves.

The unveiling of the secrets will show us the love and power of God. They will show us that the Providence of God is in charge of all things, and that we should always put our trust in Him. When these secrets are revealed, we will confidently say – *"Our Lady knew about these events and revealed them beforehand to the visionaries... she will be with us as they unfold. Let us turn to her now for guidance and place our trust in her Son."*

When all the secrets have been given to all six of the visionaries, then the apparitions will cease on a daily basis, and the secrets will begin to occur, some of which will be announced to the world (what, how, and where) three days before each occurs by the spiritual director of the visionaries (Mirjana has chosen Fr. Petar Ljubicic, O.F.M.).

The secrets are conditional. God is asking us to respond so as to avert what is coming. One example of how this occurred was when an evil that threatened the world as part of the seventh secret was eliminated through prayer and fasting. For this reason, the Blessed Virgin continues to ask for prayer and fasting. The invitation to prayer and penance is destined to ward off evil and war and above all to help save souls. Our Lady says: *"You have forgotten that* **with prayer and fasting you can ward off wars, suspend natural laws.**"

Our Lady has given ten secrets to three of the visionaries, and those visionaries no longer see her daily. The other three visionaries, as of early 2013, have received nine secrets and continue to see her and speak with her daily. When they have received the tenth secret, then the apparitions will finally end, and the secrets will begin to occur, one after the other. Our Lady is trying to prepare us with her heavenly presence and her motherly messages of love and peace.

Our Lady is giving us **a message of hope!** Let us go to Medjugorje, at least in our hearts, and draw close to our heavenly Mother, entering into her Immaculate Heart, and there, be refreshed and enlightened by her heavenly messages of hope.

So Many Graces Are Contained in These Messages

Our Lady of Medjugorje is inviting us to consecrate ourselves and our families and loved ones to her and through her to her Son, Jesus. She says:

> *Therefore, little children, I am inviting you today to* **the prayer of consecration to Jesus**, *my dear Son, so that each of your hearts may be His. And then, I am inviting you to consecration* **to my Immaculate Heart**. *I want you to consecrate yourselves as persons, as families, and as parishes so that all belongs to God through my hands.*

The messages of Medjugorje are filled with graces and hope. But, so often, everyone wants to know only about the secrets and about the future because they are curious. **But, is it not much more important to be able to influence the future events the secrets speak of?** Our Lady is telling us that we can change the course of things and she is even calling us to do so. But, how?

The Medjugorje messages ask for time of **prayer** every day, for frequent **Communion**, for monthly **confession**, for saying the **Rosary each day**, for **fasting** on bread and water on Wednesday and Friday. Don't we understand that Our Lady is asking us to do these things to help her to save the world... that these devout practices **will change the prophesied future events.**

Our Lady herself tells us:

> *I want YOU to comprehend that* **God has chosen each one of you in order to use you for the great plan of the salvation of mankind.** *YOU cannot comprehend how great your role is in God's plan.*

The Greatness of the Medjugorje Messages

Medjugorje is a 'light' set on a mountain, set there by God for all to see, especially in these times of unprecedented darkness. It is a place where Heaven and earth touched daily as Our Lady came from Heaven to appear. It is a place of miracles, especially of the soul. It is a place of divine peace; and it shows us a glimpse of what the promised soon-to-arrive Era of Peace will be like. It shows us that we can live in the spirit of the Era of Peace now, and experience the grace of daily peace now, by living the messages of Medjugorje.

Let us return to Medjugorje daily in our prayer, as Bl. Mother Teresa so recommended to her sisters and Bl. John Paul II did in his daily prayers. Let us never say that we have been to Medjugorje and gotten all it has to offer. Instead, go back to its waters and graces, and read its messages everyday. Open your hearts to the messages of Medjugorje today, and tomorrow, and the every day!

You are an important part of Our Lady's plan. And her request is for you to read her heavenly messages daily and to comprehend how important they really are. Our Lady confirms, saying:

> *There are many plans that I cannot fulfill without YOU...* **I cannot do anything without YOU***... I want to draw you closer to the Heart of Jesus. Therefore, dear little children, pray that YOU may comprehend* **the greatness of this message that I give YOU.**

New Wonders Are Coming Soon

We speculate that this book will be of much greater interest to most people after the first and maybe the second secrets have taken place. Today, hardly anyone has been interested enough to take what Our Lady is saying seriously. **Most today have lost a sense of faith** and are not even concerned about the condition of their souls as they relate to God.

But, after we experience the first two secrets, which will have been described and predicted three days before they happen, we will all then start looking for the answers for our salvation and for peace in our world. Hopefully, it will not be too late.

After the first two secrets have been revealed, and these events witnessed by the world, there will surely be a radical change in most people's perspective, especially people of the Catholic Faith. Other Christians and people of goodwill will begin looking for answers and explanations for what they must believe and what they must do in order to be saved as well. And as the secrets begin to unfold, and everyone realizes that the messages and prophecies of Medjugorje were authentic, then surely they will turn to Mary and to her heavenly messages! And there they will find hope! **This book is the book of hope.**

Mary always points to God! She asks each of us to *"make God the center of our life."* Christians, and especially Catholics, are called to evangelize and share the good news of Jesus, as the Son of God and the only Savior of all souls. They will also see with their own eyes as the secrets unfold that Jesus wants us to trust and have confidence in His Mother Mary, as she hears our prayers and intercedes before God on our behalf.

As Medjugorje continues to unfold, let us be diligent in praying for the conversion of non-believers, that they may come know and accept God and His love.

How to Respond to these Heavenly Messages

Our Lady asks for us to respond to her messages in the following **five ways**:

1. To increase our faith
2. To convert our hearts and to reconcile with God and all others
3. To pray without ceasing
4. To fast twice a week
5. To accept God's peace in our hearts, in our families, and in our world

What more specific advice is Our Lady of Medjugorje giving to us?

The messages of Medjugorje teach us that we must learn the true meaning of love – for God, and for others – and to start to live that love in our daily life. For us Catholics, Our Lady offers us some ways to best live the virtue of love today:

1. To go to confession regularly, and to confess all of your sins. No holding back! Get back in God's sanctifying grace.
2. To attend Mass frequently and pray the Mass with your heart.
3. To pray much more, especially the daily Rosary, and do so in a family setting when possible.
4. To surrender your will completely to God and make God the center of your life.
5. To ask God for His mercy (by praying the Chaplet of Divine Mercy); to be merciful to others and have confidence in God's mercy.
6. To consecrate yourself and your family to the Sacred Heart of Jesus and the Immaculate Heart of Mary.
7. To read these messages of Our Lady of Medjugorje every day and make them an active part of your life, and pray for her intentions. Then, spread these messages to others.
8. To read the Bible daily in our prayer time.

And to not delay!

Keep in mind that there are ten secrets, which will soon be revealed, and which **will occur in our lifetimes**. Some of these events will affect all of humanity. Now is the time to change the direction of your life toward God, and continue in His grace, and try to live in His Will. Then you can have every hope that your soul will be saved and that God will protect you and your loved ones. This is not the time to waver! Now is the time for a complete and serious commitment to Jesus Christ and to the messages of His Mother.

If you do not change the direction of your life, and do not embrace Jesus Christ as the Son of God, and do not live in the Will of God, then your soul may be lost for eternity. It is up to you.

We Must Live and Spread These Messages NOW!

Our mission is **to accept divine peace now and then to spread it, and to spread these heavenly messages of hope.** Our Lady of Medjugorje reminds us of how important our cooperation is, as she says:

> Dear children, **without you I am not able to help the world.** I desire that you cooperate with me in everything, even in the smallest things.

Thus, dear reader, **Our Lady is finally calling *you* to do two things**: to fully live and urgently spread these heavenly messages!

Listen as our heavenly Mother, who is being sent by God to us today, says:

> Today I am calling on you to decide whether or not you wish to **live the messages** that I am giving you. I wish you to **be active in living and spreading these messages.**

Our Lady reminds us that these messages really are from God, saying:

> **Live my messages** and put into life every word that I am giving you. May they be precious to you because **they come from Heaven.**

She is inviting us to be the new apostles of these important times. She is relying on you, as you hear her say to you:

> *Today I invite YOU to become missionaries of my messages...* *to transmit them to the whole world...* to be my joyful carriers of peace... *Through YOU, I wish to renew the world.*

Will *YOU* respond now to live and spread these heavenly messages of our times? A good way to spread these messages is to share copies of this book with others and to gather in prayer groups praying the Rosary and reading these messages. Our Lady says: *"Thank you for responding to my call."*

Our Heavenly Mother, Queen of Peace, pray for us. Amen.

❧ CHAPTER 1 ❧
ACCEPT THE LOVE OF MY SON

DECEMBER 2, 2005

"Dear children! In this holy time, allow the love and the grace of my Son to descend upon you. Only pure and merciful hearts, filled with prayer, can feel the love of my Son. Pray for those who do not have the grace to feel the love of my Son. My children, help me! Thank you."

FEBRUARY 2, 2008

"Dear children, I am with you. As a mother, I am gathering you, because I desire to erase from your hearts what I see now. Accept the love of my Son and erase fear, pain, suffering and disappointment from your heart. I have chosen you in a special way to be a light of the love of my Son. Thank you."

❧ CHAPTER 2 ❧
ACTIVE WITNESSES

FEBRUARY 25, 1997

"Dear children! Today I invite you in a special way to open yourselves to God the Creator and to become active. I invite you, little children, to see at this time who needs your spiritual or material help. By your example, little children, you will be the extended hands of God, which humanity is seeking. Only in this way will you understand, that you are called to witness and to become joyful carriers of God's word and of His love. Thank you for having responded to my call."

NOVEMBER 25, 1997

"Dear children! Today I invite you to comprehend your Christian vocation. Little children, I led and am leading you through this time of grace, that you may become conscious of your Christian vocation.
Holy martyrs died witnessing: I am a Christian and love God over everything. Little children, today also I invite you to rejoice and be joyful Christians, responsible and conscious that God called you in a special

way to be joyfully extended hands toward those who do not believe, and that through the example of your life, they may receive faith and love for God. Therefore, pray, pray, pray that your heart may open and be sensitive for the Word of God. Thank you for having responded to my call."

JUNE 25, 1999

"Dear children! Today I thank you for living and witnessing my messages with your life. Little children, be strong and pray so that prayer may give you strength and joy. Only in this way will each of you be mine and I will lead you on the way of salvation. Little children, pray and with your life witness my presence here. May each day be a joyful witness for you of God's love. Thank you for having responded to my call."

FEBRUARY 25, 2000

"Dear children! Wake up from the sleep of unbelief and sin, because this is a time of grace which God gives you. Use this time and seek the grace of healing of your heart from God, so that you may see God and man with the heart. Pray in a special way for those who have not come to know God's love, and witness with your life so that they also can come to know God and His immeasurable love. Thank you for having responded to my call."

FEBRUARY 25, 2002

"Dear children! In this time of grace, I call you to become friends of Jesus. Pray for peace in your hearts and work for your personal conversion. Little children, only in this way will you be able to become witnesses of peace and of the love of Jesus in the world. Open yourselves to prayer so that prayer becomes a need for you. Be converted, little children, and work so that as many souls as possible may come to know Jesus and His love. I am close to you and I bless you all. Thank you for having responded to my call."

SEPTEMBER 25, 2008

"Dear children! May your life, anew, be a decision for peace. Be joyful carriers of peace and do not forget that you live in a time of grace, in which God gives you great graces through my presence. Do not close yourselves, little children, but make good use of this time and seek the gift of peace and love for your life so that you may become witnesses to others. I bless you with my motherly blessing. Thank you for having responded to my call."

JUNE 25, 2009

"Dear children! Rejoice with me, convert in joy and give thanks to God for the gift of my presence among you. Pray that, in your hearts, God may be in the center of your life and with your life witness, little children, so that every creature may feel God's love. Be my extended hands for every creature, so that it may draw closer to the God of love. I bless you with my motherly blessing. Thank you for having responded to my call."

OCTOBER 25, 2009

"Dear children! Also today I bring you my blessing, I bless you all and I call you to grow on this way, which God has begun through me for your salvation. Pray, fast and joyfully witness your faith, little children, and may your heart always be filled with prayer. Thank you for having responded to my call."

MARCH 25, 2010

"Dear children! Also today I desire to call you all to be strong in prayer and in the moments when trials attack you. Live your Christian vocation in joy and humility and witness to everyone. I am with you and I carry you all before my Son Jesus, and He will be your strength and support. Thank you for having responded to my call."

FEBRUARY 25, 2011

"Dear children! Nature is awakening and on the trees the first buds are seen which will bring most beautiful flowers and fruit. I desire that you also, little children, work on your conversion and that you be those who witness with their life, so that your example may be a sign and an incentive for conversion to others. I am with you and before my Son Jesus I intercede for your conversion. Thank you for having responded to my call."

APRIL 25, 2011

"Dear children! As nature gives the most beautiful colors of the year, I also call you to witness with your life and to help others to draw closer to my Immaculate Heart, so that the flame of love for the Most High may sprout in their hearts. I am with you and I unceasingly pray for you that your life may be a reflection of Heaven here on earth. Thank you for having responded to my call."

SEPTEMBER 25, 2011

"Dear children! I call you, for this time to be for all of you, a time of witnessing. You, who live in the love of God and have experienced His gifts, witness them with your words and life that they may be for the joy and encouragement to others in faith. I am with you and incessantly intercede before God for all of you that your faith may always be alive and joyful, and in the love of God. Thank you for having responded to my call."

❧ CHAPTER 3 ❧
AN INCENTIVE FOR THE GOOD

MARCH 25, 2004

"Dear children! Also today, I call you to open yourselves to prayer. Especially now, in this time of grace, open your hearts, little children, and express your love to the Crucified. Only in this way, will you discover peace, and prayer will begin to flow from your heart into the world. Be an example, little children, and an incentive for the good. I am close to you and I love you all. Thank you for having responded to my call."

❧ CHAPTER 4 ❧
ARE YOU WITH ME

APRIL 2, 2008

"Dear children! Also today, as I am with you in the great love of God, I desire to ask you: Are you with me? Is your heart open for me? Do you permit me to purify and prepare it for my Son? My children, you are chosen because, in your time, the great grace of God descended on earth. Do not hesitate to accept it. Thank you."

ঔ CHAPTER 5 ৬

AS A MOTHER, I FIGHT FOR YOU

JANUARY 2, 2008

"Dear children! With all the strength of my heart, I love you and give myself to you. As a mother fights for her children, I pray for you and fight for you. I ask you not to be afraid to open yourselves, so as to be able to love with the heart and give yourselves to others. The more that you do this with the heart, the more you will receive and the better you will understand my Son and His gift to you. May everyone recognize you through the love of my Son and through me. Thank you."

ঔ CHAPTER 6 ৬

AS NEVER UP TO NOW

APRIL 4, 1985 (HOLY THURSDAY)

"Dear children! I thank you for having started to think more about God's glory in your hearts. Today is the day when I wished to stop giving the messages because some individuals did not accept me. The parish has been moved and I wish to keep on giving you messages as it has never been in history from the beginning of the world. Thank you for having responded to my call."

FEBRUARY 25, 2004

"Dear children! Also today, as never up to now, I call you to open your hearts to my messages. Little children, be those who draw souls to God and not those who distance them. I am with you and love you all with a special love. This is a time of penance and conversion. From the bottom of my heart, I call you to be mine with all your heart and then you will see that your God is great, because He will give you an abundance of blessings and peace. Thank you for having responded to my call."

❧ CHAPTER 7 ❦
BLESSED OBJECTS

JULY 18, 1985

"Dear children! Today I call you to place more blessed objects in your homes and that everyone put some blessed objects on their person. Bless all the objects and thus Satan will attack you less because you will have armor against him. Thank you for having responded to my call."

❧ CHAPTER 8 ❦
CHANGE DIRECTION OF YOUR LIFE

MAY 25, 1990

"Dear children! I invite you to decide with seriousness to live this novena. Consecrate the time to prayer and to sacrifice. I am with you and I desire to help you to grow in renunciation and mortification, that you may be able to understand the beauty of the life of people who go on giving themselves to me in special way. Dear children, God blesses you day after day and desires a change of your life. Therefore, pray that you may have the strength to change your life. Thank you for having responded to my call."

MARCH 25, 1990

"Dear children! I am with you even if you are not conscious of it. I want to protect you from everything that Satan offers you and through which he wants to destroy you. As I bore Jesus in my womb, so also, dear children, do I wish to bear you into holiness. God wants to save you and sends you messages through men, nature, and so many things which can only help you to understand that you must change the direction of your life. Therefore, little children, understand also the greatness of the gift which God is giving you through me, so that I may protect you with my mantle and lead you to the joy of life. Thank you for having responded to my call."

OCTOBER 25, 1992

"Dear children! I invite you to prayer now when Satan is strong and wishes to make as many souls as possible his own. Pray, dear children, and have more trust in me because I am here in order to help you and to guide you on a new path toward a new life. Therefore, dear little children, listen and live what I tell you because it is important for you when I shall not be with you any longer that you remember my words and all that I told you. I call you to begin to change your life from the beginning and that you decide for conversion not with words but with your life. Thank you for having responded to my call."

❧ CHAPTER 9 ❧
CHRISTIAN UNITY

JANUARY 25, 2005

"Dear children! In this time of grace again I call you to prayer. Pray, little children, for unity of Christians, that all may be one heart. Unity will really be among you inasmuch as you will pray and forgive. Do not forget: love will conquer only if you pray, and your heart will open. Thank you for having responded to my call."

❧ CHAPTER 10 ❧
CHRISTMAS

DECEMBER 21, 1984 (FRIDAY)

"I want you to be a flower which will blossom for Jesus on Christmas. And a flower that will not stop blooming when Christmas is over. I want your hearts to be shepherds to Jesus." (Message given through Jelena Vasilj)

DECEMBER 5, 1985

"Dear children! I am calling you to prepare yourselves for Christmas by means of penance, prayer and works of charity. Dear children, do not look toward material things, because then you will not be able to experience Christmas. Thank you for having responded to my call."

JANUARY 2, 2006

"Dear children, my Son is born. Your Savior is here with you. What prevents your heart from receiving Him? What all is false within them? Purify them by fasting and prayer. Recognize and receive my Son. He alone gives you true peace and true love. The way to eternal life is He – my Son. Thank you"

DECEMBER 25, 2008

"Dear children! You are running, working, gathering – but without blessing. You are not praying! Today I call you to stop in front of the manger and to meditate on Jesus, Whom I give to you today also, to bless you and to help you to comprehend that, without Him, you have no future. Therefore, little children, surrender your lives into the hands of Jesus, for Him to lead you and protect you from every evil. Thank you for having responded to my call."

DECEMBER 25, 2009

"Dear children! On this joyful day, I bring all of you before my Son, the King of Peace, that He may give you His peace and blessing. Little children, in love share that peace and blessing with others. Thank you for having responded to my call."

❧ CHAPTER 11 ❧
CLEAN HEART

OCTOBER 17, 1985

"Dear children! Everything has its own time. Today I call you to start working on your own hearts. Now that all the work in the field is over, you are finding time for cleaning even the most neglected areas, but you leave your heart aside. Work more and clean with love every part of your heart. Thank you for having responded to my call."

MARCH 18, 2004

The visionary Mirjana Dragicevic-Soldo had daily apparitions from June 24, 1981 to December 25, 1982. During the last daily apparition, Our Lady gave her the 10th secret, and told her that she would appear to her once a year, on the 18th of March. It has been this way through the years. This year several thousand pilgrims gathered to pray the Rosary at the Cenacolo Community in Medjugorje. The apparition lasted from 13:58 to 14:03 and Our Lady gave the following message:

"Dear children! Also today, watching you with a heart full of love, I desire to tell you that what you persistently seek, what you long for, my little children, is before you. It is sufficient that, in a cleaned heart, you place my Son in the first place, and then you will be able to see. Listen to me and permit me to lead you to this in a motherly way."

☙ CHAPTER 12 ❧
CONFESSION

MARCH 24, 1985 (SUNDAY)

"Today I wish to call you all to confession, even if you have confessed a few days ago. I wish that you all experience my feast day within yourselves. But you cannot experience it unless you abandon yourselves completely to God. Therefore, I am inviting you all to reconciliation with God!"

FEBRUARY 25, 1987

"Dear children! Today I want to wrap you all in my mantle and lead you all along the way of conversion. Dear children, I beseech you, surrender to the Lord your entire past, all the evil that has accumulated in your hearts. I want each one of you to be happy, but in sin nobody can be happy. Therefore, dear children, pray, and in prayer you shall realize a new way of joy. Joy will manifest in your hearts and thus you shall be joyful witnesses of that which I and My Son want from each one of you. I am blessing you. Thank you for having responded to my call."

JANUARY 25, 1995

"Dear children! I invite you to open the door of your heart to Jesus as the flower opens itself to the sun. Jesus desires to fill your hearts with peace and joy. You cannot, little children, realize peace if you are not at peace with Jesus. Therefore, I invite you to confession so Jesus may be your truth and peace. So, little children, pray to have the strength to realize what I am telling you. I am with you and I love you. Thank you for having responded to my call."

NOVEMBER 25, 1998

"Dear children! Today I call you to prepare yourselves for the coming of Jesus. In a special way, prepare your hearts. May holy Confession be the first act of conversion for you and then, dear children, decide for holiness. May your conversion and decision for holiness begin today and not tomorrow. Little children, I call you all to the way of salvation and I desire to show you the way to Heaven. That is why, little children, be mine and decide with me for holiness. Little children, accept prayer with seriousness and pray, pray, pray. Thank you for having responded to my call."

NOVEMBER 25, 2002

"Dear children! I call you also today to conversion. Open your heart to God, little children, through Holy Confession and prepare your soul so that little Jesus can be born anew in your heart. Permit Him to transform you and lead you on the way of peace and joy. Little children, decide for prayer. Especially now, in this time of grace, may your heart yearn for prayer. I am close to you and intercede before God for all of you. Thank you for having responded to my call."

FEBRUARY 25, 2007

"Dear children! Open your heart to God's mercy in this Lenten time. The Heavenly Father desires to deliver each of you from the slavery of sin. Therefore, little children, make good use of this time and through meeting with God in confession, leave sin and decide for holiness. Do this out of love for Jesus, who redeemed you all with his blood, that you may be happy and in peace. Do not forget, little children: your freedom is your weakness; therefore, follow my messages with seriousness. Thank you for having responded to my call."

JULY 2, 2007

"Dear children! In the great love of God, I come to you today to lead you on the way of humility and meekness. The first station on that way, my children, is confession. Reject your arrogance and kneel down before my Son. Comprehend, my children, that you have nothing and you can do nothing. The only thing that is yours and what you possess is sin. Be cleansed and accept meekness and humility. My Son could have won with strength, but He chose meekness, humility and love. Follow my Son and give me your hands so that, together, we may climb the mountain and win. Thank you."

FEBRUARY 25, 2009

"Dear children! In this time of renunciation, prayer and penance, I call you anew: go and confess your sins so that grace may open your hearts, and permit it to change you. Convert little children, open yourselves to God and to His plan for each of you. Thank you for having responded to my call."

MAY 2, 2011

"Dear children; God the Father is sending me to show you the way of salvation, because He, my children, desires to save you and not to condemn you. That is why I, as a mother, am gathering you around me, because with my motherly love I desire to help you to be free of the dirtiness of the past and to begin to live anew and differently. I am calling you to resurrect in my Son. Along with confession of sins renounce everything that has distanced you from my Son and that has made your life empty and unsuccessful. Say 'yes' to the Father with the heart and set out on the way of salvation to which He is calling you through the Holy Spirit. Thank you. I am especially praying for the shepherds (priests), for God to help them to be alongside you with a fullness of heart."

❧ CHAPTER 13 ❦

CONSECRATION TO MARY AND JESUS

NOVEMBER 27, 1986

"Dear children! Again today I call you to consecrate your life to me with love, so I am able to guide you with love. I love you, dear children, with a special love and I desire to bring you all to Heaven unto God. I want you to realize that this life lasts briefly compared to the one in Heaven. Therefore, dear children, decide again today for God. Only that way will I be able to show how much you are dear to me and how much I desire all to be saved and to be with me in Heaven. Thank you for having responded to my call."

OCTOBER 25, 1988

"Dear children! My invitation that you live the messages which I am giving you is a daily one, especially, little children, because I want to draw you closer to the Heart of Jesus. Therefore, little children, I am inviting you today to the prayer of consecration to Jesus, my dear Son, so that each of you may be His. And then I am inviting you to the consecration of my Immaculate Heart. I want you to consecrate yourselves as parents, as families and as parishioners so that all belong to God through my heart. Therefore, little children, pray that you comprehend the greatness of this message which I am giving you. I do not want anything for myself, rather all for the salvation of your soul. Satan is strong and therefore, you, little children, by constant prayer, press tightly against my motherly heart. Thank you for having responded to my call."

OCTOBER 25, 2003

"Dear children! I call you anew to consecrate yourselves to my heart and the heart of my Son Jesus. I desire, little children, to lead you all on the way of conversion and holiness. Only in this way, through you, we can lead all the more souls on the way of salvation. Do not delay, little children, but say with all your heart: "I want to help Jesus and Mary that all the more brothers and sisters may come to know the way of holiness.

In this way, you will feel the contentment of being friends of Jesus. Thank you for having responded to my call."

MAY 25, 2004
"Dear children! Also today, I urge you to consecrate yourselves to my Heart and to the Heart of my Son Jesus. Only in this way will you be mine more each day and you will inspire each other all the more to holiness. In this way joy will rule your hearts and you will be carriers of peace and love. Thank you for having responded to my call."

Consecration to the Sacred Heart of Jesus

Adorable Heart of Jesus, the tenderest, the most amiable, the most generous of all hearts, penetrated with gratitude at the sight of Your benefits, I come to consecrate myself wholly and unreservedly to You! I wish to devote all my energies to propagating Your worship and winning, if possible, all hearts to You. Receive my heart this day, O Jesus! Or rather take it, change it, purify it, to render it worthy of You; Make it humble, gentle, patient, faithful and generous like Yours, by inflaming it with the fire of Your love. Hide it in Your Divine Heart with all hearts that love You and are consecrated to You; never permit me to take my heart from You again. Let me rather die than grieve Your Adorable Heart. You know O Heart of Jesus, that the desire of my heart is to love You always, to be wholly Yours in life and in death, in time and eternity. Most Sacred Heart of Jesus, have mercy on us. Sacred Heart of Jesus, I trust in You.

Consecration to
the Immaculate Heart of Mary

I, (Name), a faithless sinner, renew and ratify today in your hands, O Immaculate Mother, the vows of my baptism. I renounce forever Satan, his pomps and works; and I give myself entirely to Jesus Christ, the Incarnate Wisdom, to carry my cross after Him all the days of my life, and to be more faithful to Him than I have ever been before.

In the presence of all the heavenly court I choose you this day, for my Mother and Mistress. I deliver and consecrate to you, as your slave, my body and soul, my goods, both interior and exterior, and even the value of all my good actions, past, present and future; leaving to you the entire and full right of disposing of me, and all that belongs to me, without exception, according to your good pleasure, for the greater glory of God, in time and in eternity. Amen.

❧ CHAPTER 14 ❧
CONVERSION OF YOUR HEART

JANUARY 23, 1986

"Dear children! Again I call you to prayer with the heart. If you pray with the heart, dear children, the ice of your brothers will melt and every barrier shall disappear. Conversion will be easy for all who desire to accept it. That is the gift which by prayer you must obtain for your neighbor. Thank you for having responded to my call."

JANUARY 25, 1988

"Dear children! Today again I am calling you to complete conversion, which is difficult for those who have not chosen God. God can give you everything that you seek from Him. But you seek God only when sicknesses, problems and difficulties come to you and you think that God is far from you and is not listening and does not hear your prayers. No, dear children, that is not the truth. When you are far from God, you cannot receive graces because you do not seek them with a firm faith. Day by day, I am praying for you, and I want to draw you ever more near to God, but I cannot if you don't want it. Therefore, dear children put your life in God's hands. I bless you all. Thank you for having responded to my call."

JUNE 25, 1992

"Dear children! Today I am happy, even if in my heart there is still a little sadness for all those who have started on this path and then have left it. My presence here is to take you on a new path, the path to salvation. This is why I call you, day after day to conversion. But if you do not pray, you cannot say that you are on the way to being converted. I pray for you and I intercede to God for peace; first peace in your hearts and also peace around you, so that God may be your peace. Thank you for having responded to my call."

SEPTEMBER 25, 1998

"Dear children! Today, I call you to become my witnesses by living the faith of your fathers. Little children, you seek signs and messages and do not see that, with every morning sunrise, God calls you to convert and to return to the way of truth and salvation. You speak much, little children, but you work little on your conversion. That is why, convert and start to live my messages, not with your words but with your life. In this way, little children, you will have the strength to decide for the true conversion of the heart. Thank you for having responded to my call."

APRIL 25, 2000

"Dear children! Also today I call you to conversion. You are concerned too much about material things and little about spiritual ones. Open your hearts and start again to work more on your personal conversion. Decide everyday to dedicate time to God and to prayer until prayer becomes a joyful meeting with God for you. Only in this way will your life have meaning and with joy you will contemplate eternal life. Thank you for having responded to my call."

ANNUAL APPARITION TO JAKOV ON DECEMBER 25, 2001

At the last daily apparition to Jakov Colo on September 12, 1998, Our Lady told him that henceforth he would have one apparition a year, every December 25, on Christmas Day. This is also how it was this year. The apparition began at 3:30 pm and lasted 5 minutes. Our Lady gave the following message:

"Dear Children, today when Jesus is born anew for you, in a special way, I want to call you to conversion. Pray, pray, pray for the conversion of your heart, so that Jesus may be born in you all and may dwell in you and come to reign over your entire being. Thank you for having responded to the call."

APRIL 25, 2002

"Dear children! Rejoice with me in this time of spring when all nature is awakening and your hearts long for change. Open yourselves, little children, and pray. Do not forget that I am with you and I desire to take you all to my Son that He may give you the gift of sincere love towards God and everything that is from Him. Open yourselves to prayer and seek a conversion of your hearts from God; everything else He sees and provides. Thank you for having responded to my call."

AUGUST 25, 2004

"Dear children! I call you all to conversion of heart. Decide, as in the first days of my coming here, for a complete change of your life. In this way, little children, you will have the strength to kneel and to open your hearts before God. God will hear your prayers and answer them. Before God, I intercede for each of you. Thank you for having responded to my call."

AUGUST 25, 2007

"Dear Children! Also today I call you to conversion. May Your Life, little children, be a reflection of God's goodness and not of hatred and unfaithfulness. Pray, little children, that prayer may become life for you. In this way, in your life you will discover the peace and joy which God gives to those who have an open heart to his love. And you who are far from God's mercy, convert so that God may not become deaf to your prayers and that it may not be too late for you. Therefore, in this time of grace, convert and put God in the first place in your life. Thank you for having responded to my call."

AUGUST 25, 2008

"Dear children! Also today I call you to personal conversion. You be those who will convert and, with your life, will witness, love, forgive and bring the joy of the Risen One into this world, where my Son died and where people do not feel a need to seek Him and to discover Him in their lives. You adore Him, and may your hope be hope to those hearts who do not have Jesus. Thank you for having responded to my call."

SEPTEMBER 25, 2010

"Dear children! Today I am with you and bless you all with my motherly blessing of peace, and I urge you to live your life of faith even more, because you are still weak and are not humble. I urge you, little children, to speak less and to work more on your personal conversion so that your witness may be fruitful. And may your life be unceasing prayer. Thank you for having responded to my call."

☙ CHAPTER 15 ❧
CONVERSION OF SINNERS

OCTOBER 8, 1984 (MONDAY)
(JAKOV WAS SICK AND RECEIVED THIS message at home.)
"Dear children, Let all the prayers you say in your homes in the evening be for the conversion of sinners because the world is in great sin. Every evening pray the Rosary."

MARCH 25, 1999
"Dear children! I call you to prayer with the heart. In a special way, little children, I call you to pray for conversion of sinners, for those who pierce my heart and the heart of my Son Jesus with the sword of hatred and daily blasphemies. Let us pray, little children, for all those who do not desire to come to know the love of God, even though they are in the Church. Let us pray that they convert, so that the Church may resurrect in love. Only with love and prayer, little children, can you live this time which is given to you for conversion. Place God in the first place, then the risen Jesus will become your friend. Thank you for having responded to my call."

☙ CHAPTER 16 ❧
DECIDE FOR HEAVEN

NOVEMBER 6, 1986
"Dear children! Today I wish to call you to pray daily for souls in purgatory. For every soul prayer and grace is necessary to reach God and the love of God. By doing this, dear children, you obtain new intercessors who will help you in life to realize that all the earthly things are not important for you, that only Heaven is that for which it is necessary to strive. Therefore, dear children, pray without ceasing that you may be able to help yourselves and the others to whom your prayers will bring joy. Thank you for having responded to my call."

NOVEMBER 27, 1986

"Dear children! Again today I call you to consecrate your life to me with love, so I am able to guide you with love. I love you, dear children, with a special love and I desire to bring you all to Heaven unto God. I want you to realize that this life lasts briefly compared to the one in Heaven. Therefore, dear children, decide again today for God. Only that way will I be able to show how much you are dear to me and how much I desire all to be saved and to be with me in Heaven. Thank you for having responded to my call."

JULY 25, 1987

"Dear children! I beseech you to take up the way of holiness beginning today. I love you and, therefore, I want you to be holy. I do not want Satan to block you on that way. Dear children, pray and accept all that God is offering you on a way which is bitter. But at the same time, God will reveal every sweetness to whomever begins to go on that way, and He will gladly answer every call of God. Do not attribute importance to petty things. Long for Heaven. Thank you for having responded to my call."

OCTOBER 25, 1987

"My dear children! Today I want to call all of you to decide for Paradise. The way is difficult for those who have not decided for God. Dear children, decide and believe that God is offering Himself to you in His fullness. You are invited and you need to answer the call of the Father, Who is calling you through me. Pray, because in prayer each one of you will be able to achieve complete love. I am blessing you and I desire to help you so that each one of you might be under my motherly mantle. Thank you for having responded to my call."

AUGUST 25, 1998

"Dear children! Today I invite you to come still closer to me through prayer. Little children, I am your mother, I love you and I desire that each of you be saved and thus be with me in Heaven. That is why, little children, pray, pray, pray until your life becomes prayer. Thank you for having responded to my call."

MARCH 25, 2007

"Dear children! I desire to thank you from my heart for your Lenten renunciations. I desire to inspire you to continue to live fasting with an open heart. By fasting and renunciation, little children, you will be stronger in faith. In God you will find true peace through daily prayer. I am with you and I am not tired. I desire to take you all with me to Heaven, therefore, decide daily for holiness. Thank you for having responded to my call."

❧ CHAPTER 17 ❧
DO NOT ATTEMPT TO HAVE FAMILIES AND SOCIETIES WITHOUT GOD THE FATHER

OCTOBER 2, 2011

"Dear children; Also today my motherly heart calls you to prayer, to your personal relationship with God the Father, to the joy of prayer in Him. God the Father is not far away from you and He is not unknown to you. He revealed Himself to you through my Son and gave you Life that is my Son. Therefore, my children, do not give in to temptations that want to separate you from God the Father. Pray! Do not attempt to have families and societies without Him. Pray! Pray that your hearts may be flooded with the goodness which comes only from my Son, Who is sincere goodness. Only hearts filled with goodness can comprehend and accept God the Father. I will continue to lead you. In a special way I implore you not to judge your shepherds. My children, are you forgetting that God the Father called them? Pray! Thank you."

❧ CHAPTER 18 ❧
DO NOT BE DEAF (TO MY CALL)

SEPTEMBER 25, 2003

"Dear children! Also today I call you to come closer to my heart. Only in this way, will you comprehend the gift of my presence here among you. I desire, little children, to lead you to the heart of my Son Jesus; but you resist and do not desire to open your hearts to prayer. Again, little children, I call you not to be deaf but to comprehend my call, which is salvation for you. Thank you for having responded to my call."

❧ CHAPTER 19 ❧
DO NOT REFUSE MY LOVE

AUGUST 2, 2009

"Dear children! I am coming, with my motherly love, to point out the way by which you are to set out, in order that you may be all the more like my Son; and by that, closer to and more pleasing to God. Do not refuse my love. Do not renounce salvation and eternal life for the sake of transience and frivolity of this life. I am among you to lead you and, as a mother, to caution you. Come with me."

❧ CHAPTER 20 ❧
ETERNITY AND ETERNAL LIFE

JANUARY 2, 2006

"Dear children, my Son is born. Your Savior is here with you. What prevents your heart from receiving Him? What all is false within them? Purify them by fasting and prayer. Recognize and receive my Son. He alone gives you true peace and true love. The way to eternal life is He – my Son. Thank you."

OCTOBER 25, 2006

"Dear children! Today the Lord permitted me to tell you again that you live in a time of grace. You are not conscious, little children, that God is giving you a great opportunity to convert and to live in peace and love. You are so blind and attached to earthly things and think of earthly life. God sent me to lead you toward eternal life. I, little children, am not tired, although I see that your hearts are heavy and tired for everything that is a grace and a gift. Thank you for having responded to my call."

NOVEMBER 25, 2006

"Dear children! Also today I call you to pray, pray, pray. Little children, when you pray you are close to God and He gives you the desire for eternity. This is a time when you can speak more about God and do more for God. Therefore, little children, do not resist but permit Him to lead you, to change you and to enter into your life. Do not forget that you are travelers on the way toward eternity. Therefore, little children, permit God to lead you as a shepherd leads his flock. Thank you for having responded to my call."

JANUARY 25, 2009

"Dear children! Also today I call you to prayer. May prayer be for you like the seed that you will put in my heart, which I will give over to my Son Jesus for you, for the salvation of your souls. I desire, little children, for each of you to fall in love with eternal life which is your future, and for all worldly things to be a help for you to draw you closer to God the Creator. I am with you for this long because you are on the wrong path. Only with my help, little children, you will open your eyes. There are many of those who, by living my messages, comprehend that they are on the way of holiness towards eternity. Thank you for having responded to my call."

SEPTEMBER 25, 2009

"Dear children, with joy, persistently work on your conversion. Offer all your joys and sorrows to my Immaculate Heart that I may lead you all to my most beloved Son, so that you may find joy in His Heart. I am with you to instruct you and to lead you towards eternity. Thank you for having responded to my call."

DECEMBER 25, 2009

"Dear children! All of this time in which God in a special way permits me to be with you, I desire to lead you on the way that leads to Jesus and to your salvation. My little children, you can find salvation only in God and therefore, especially on this day of grace with little Jesus in my arms, I call you to permit Jesus to be born in your hearts. Only with Jesus in your heart can you set out on the way of salvation and eternal life. Thank you for having responded to my call."

❧ CHAPTER 21 ❧
EUCHARISTIC ADORATION

MARCH 15, 1984

"Tonight also, dear children, I am grateful to you in a special way for being here. Unceasingly adore the Most Blessed Sacrament of the Altar. I am always present when the faithful are adoring. Special graces are then being received."

SEPTEMBER 25, 1995

"Dear Children! Today I invite you to fall in love with the Most Holy Sacrament of the Altar. Adore Him, little children, in your Parishes and in this way you will be united with the entire world. Jesus will become your friend and you will not talk of Him like someone whom you barely know. Unity with Him will be a joy for you and you will become witnesses to the love of Jesus that He has for every creature. Little children, when you adore Jesus you are also close to me. Thank you for having responded to my call."

MARCH 25, 2008

"Dear children! I call you to work on your personal conversion. You are still far from meeting with God in your heart. Therefore, spend all the more time in prayer and Adoration of Jesus in the Most Blessed Sacrament of the Altar, for Him to change you and to put into your hearts a living faith and a desire for eternal life. Everything is passing, little children, only God is not passing. I am with you and I encourage you with love. Thank you for having responded to my call."

JULY 2, 2009

"Dear children! I am calling you because I need you. I need hearts ready for immeasurable love – hearts that are not burdened by vanity – hearts that are ready to love as my Son loved – that are ready to sacrifice themselves as my Son sacrificed himself. I need you. In order to come with me, forgive yourselves, forgive others and adore my Son. Adore him also for those who have not come to know him, those who do not love him. Therefore, I need you; therefore, I call you. Thank you."

❧ CHAPTER 22 ❧
FAITH

APRIL 25, 1988

"Dear children! God wants to make you holy. Therefore, through me He is inviting you to complete surrender. Let holy mass be your life. Understand that the church is God's palace, the place in which I gather you and want to show you the way to God. Come and pray. Neither look at others nor slander them, but rather, let your life be a testimony on the way of holiness. Churches deserve respect and are set apart as holy because God, who became man, dwells in them day and night. Therefore, little children, believe and pray that the Father increase your faith, and then ask for whatever you need. I am with you and I am rejoicing because of you conversion and I am protecting you with my motherly mantle. Thank you for having responded to my call."

MARCH 25, 1995

"Dear Children! Today I invite you to live the peace in your hearts and families. There is no peace, little children, where there is no prayer and there is no love, where there is no faith. Therefore, little children, I invite you all, to decide again today for conversion. I am close to you and I invite you all, little children, into my embrace to help you, but you do not want and in this way, Satan is tempting you, and in the smallest thing, your faith disappears. This is why little children, pray and through prayer, you will have blessing and peace.   Thank you for having responded to my call."

AUGUST 25, 2002

"Dear children! Also today I am with you in prayer so that God gives you an even stronger faith. Little children, your faith is small and you are not even aware how much, despite this, you are not ready to seek the gift of faith from God. That is why I am with you, little children, to help you comprehend my messages and put them into life. Pray, pray, pray and only in faith and through prayer your soul will find peace and the world will find joy to be with God. Thank you for having responded to my call."

NOVEMBER 25, 2005

"Dear children! Also today I call you to pray, pray, pray until prayer becomes life for you. Little children, at this time, in a special way, I pray before God to give you the gift of faith. Only in faith will you discover the joy of the gift of life that God has given you. Your heart will be joyful thinking of eternity. I am with you and love you with a tender love. Thank you for having responded to my call."

OCTOBER 2, 2007

"Dear children, I call you to accompany me in my mission of God with an open heart and complete trust. The way on which I lead you, to God, is difficult but persevering and in the end we will all rejoice through God. Therefore, my children, do not stop praying for the gift of faith. Only through faith will the Word of God be light in this darkness which desires to envelop us. Do not be afraid, I am with you. Thank you."

❧ CHAPTER 23 ❧
FAMILY PRAYER

NOVEMBER 1, 1984

"Dear children! Today I call you to the renewal of prayer in your homes. The work in the fields is over. Now devote yourselves to prayer. Let prayer take the first place in your families. Thank you for having responded to my call."

DECEMBER 6, 1984

"Dear children! These days I am calling you to family prayer. In God's Name many times I have been giving you messages, but you have not listened to me. This Christmas will be unforgettable for you only if you accept the messages which I am giving you. Dear children, don't allow that day of joy to become my most sorrowful day. Thank you for having responded to my call."

MAY 1, 1986

"Dear children! I beseech you to start changing your life in the family. Let the family be a harmonious flower that I wish to give to Jesus. Dear children, let every family be active in prayer for I wish that the fruits in the family be seen one day. Only that way shall I give you all, like petals, as a gift to Jesus in fulfillment of God's plans. Thank you for having responded to my call."

JULY 24, 1986

"Dear children! I rejoice because of all of you who are on the way of holiness and I beseech you, by your own testimony help those who do not know how to live in holiness. Therefore, dear children, let your family be a place where holiness is birthed. Help everyone to live in holiness, but especially your own family. Thank you for having responded to my call."

JANUARY 25, 1992

"Dear Children! Today, I am inviting you to a renewal of prayer in your families so that way every family will become a joy to my son Jesus. Therefore, dear children, pray and seek more time for Jesus and then you will be able to understand and accept everything, even the most difficult sicknesses and crosses. I am with you and I desire to take you into my heart and protect you, but you have not yet decided. Therefore, dear children, I am seeking for you to pray, so through prayer you would allow me to help you. Pray, my dear little children, so prayer becomes your daily bread. Thank you for having responded to my call."

AUGUST 25, 1995

"Dear children! Today I invite you to prayer. Let prayer be life for you. A family cannot say that it is in peace if it does not pray. Therefore, let your morning begin with morning prayer, and the evening end with thanksgiving. Little children, I am with you, and I love you and I bless you and I wish for every one of you to be in my embrace. You cannot be in my embrace if you are not ready to pray every day. Thank you for having responded to my call."

APRIL 25, 1996

"Dear children! Today I invite you again to put prayer in the first place in your families. Little children, when God is in the first place, then you will, in all that you do, seek the will of God. In this way your daily conversion will become easier. Little children, seek with humility that which is not in order in your hearts, and you shall understand what you have to do. Conversion will become a daily duty that you will do with joy. Little children, I am with you, I bless you all and I invite you to become my witnesses by prayer and personal conversion. Thank you for having responded to my call."

MAY 25, 1997

"Dear children! Today I invite you to glorify God and for the Name of God to be holy in your hearts and in your life. Little children, when you are in the holiness of God, He is with you and gives you peace and joy which come only from God through prayer. That is why, little children, renew prayer in your families and your heart will glorify the holy Name of God and heaven will reign in your heart. I am close to you and I intercede for you before God. Thank you for having responded to my call."

SEPTEMBER 25, 1999

"Dear children! Today again I call you to become carriers of my peace. In a special way, now when it is being said that God is far away, He has truly never been nearer to you. I call you to renew prayer in your families by reading the Sacred Scripture and to experience joy in meeting with God who infinitely loves His creatures. Thank you for having responded to my call."

NOVEMBER 25, 2009

"Dear children! In this time of grace I call you all to renew prayer in your families. Prepare yourselves with joy for the coming of Jesus. Little children, may your hearts be pure and pleasing, so that love and warmth may flow through you into every heart that is far from His love. Little children, be my extended hands, hands of love for all those who have become lost, who have no more faith and hope. Thank you for having responded to my call."

&~ CHAPTER 24 ~&
FASTING

SEPTEMBER 20, 1984

"Dear children! Today I call on you to begin fasting with the heart. There are many people who are fasting, but only because everyone else is fasting. It has become a custom which no one wants to stop. I ask the parish to fast out of gratitude because God has allowed me to stay this long in this parish. Dear children, fast and pray with the heart. Thank you for having responded to my call."

SEPTEMBER 26, 1985

"Dear children! I thank you for all the prayers. Thank you for all the sacrifices. I wish to tell you, dear children, to renew the messages which I am giving you. Especially live the fast, because by fasting you will achieve and cause me the joy of the whole plan, which God is planning here in Medjugorje, being fulfilled. Thank you for having responded to my call."

SEPTEMBER 4, 1986

"Dear children! Today again I am calling you to prayer and fasting. You know, dear children, that with your help I am able to accomplish everything and force Satan not to be seducing to evil and to remove himself from this place. Dear children, Satan is lurking for each individual. Especially in everyday affairs he wants to spread confusion among each one of you. Therefore, dear children, my call to you is that your day would be only prayer and complete surrender to God. Thank you for having responded to my call."

JULY 25, 1991

"Dear Children! Today I invite you to pray for peace. At this time peace is being threatened in a special way, and I am seeking from you to renew fasting and prayer in your families. Dear children, I desire you to grasp the seriousness of the situation and that much of what will happen depends on your prayers and you are praying a little bit. Dear children, I am with you and I am inviting you to begin to pray and fast seriously as in the first days of my coming. Thank you for having responded to my call."

NOVEMBER 25, 1996

"Dear children! Today, again, I invite you to pray, so that through prayer, fasting and small sacrifices you may prepare yourselves for the coming of Jesus. May this time, little children, be a time of grace for you. Use every moment and do good, for only in this way will you feel the birth of Jesus in your hearts. If with your life you give an example and become a sign of God's love, joy will prevail in the hearts of men. Thank you for having responded to my call."

MARCH 25, 1998

"Dear children! Also today I call you to fasting and renunciation. Little children, renounce that which hinders you from being closer to Jesus. In a special way I call you: Pray, because only through prayer will you be able to overcome your will and discover the will of God even in the smallest things. By your daily life, little children, you will become an example and witness that you live for Jesus or against Him and His will. Little children, I desire that you become apostles of love. By loving, little children, it will be recognized that you are mine. Thank you for having responded to my call."

APRIL 25, 1999

"Dear children! Also today I call you to prayer. Little children, be joyful carriers of peace and love in this peaceless world. By fasting and prayer, witness that you are mine and that you live my messages. Pray and seek! I am praying and interceding for you before God that you convert; that your life and behavior always be Christian.   Thank you for having responded to my call."

JANUARY 25, 2001

"Dear children! Today I call you to renew prayer and fasting with even greater enthusiasm until prayer becomes a joy for you.   Little children, the one who prays is not afraid of the future and the one who fasts is not afraid of evil.   Once again, I repeat to you: only through prayer and fasting also wars can be stopped. wars of your unbelief and fear for the future. I am with you and am teaching you little children: your peace and hope are in God. That is why draw closer to God and put Him in the first place in your life. Thank you for having responded to my call."

FEBRUARY 25, 2003

"Dear children! Also today I call you to pray and fast for peace. As I have already said and now repeat to you, little children, only with prayer and fasting can wars also be stopped. Peace is a precious gift from God. Seek, pray and you will receive it. Speak about peace and carry peace in your hearts. Nurture it like a flower which is in need of water, tenderness and light. Be those who carry peace to others. I am with you and intercede for all of you. Thank you for having responded to my call."

MARCH 25, 2007

"Dear children! I desire to thank you from my heart for your Lenten renunciations. I desire to inspire you to continue to live fasting with an open heart. By fasting and renunciation, little children, you will be stronger in faith. In God you will find true peace through daily prayer. I am with you and I am not tired. I desire to take you all with me to Heaven, therefore, decide daily for holiness. Thank you for having responded to my call."

JUNE 2, 2010

"Dear Children! Today I call you with prayer and fasting to clear the path in which my Son will enter into your hearts. Accept me as a mother and a messenger of God's love and His desire for your salvation. Free yourself of everything from the past which burdens you, that gives you a sense of guilt, that which previously led you astray in error and darkness.

Accept the light. Be born anew in the righteousness of my Son. Thank you."

❧ CHAPTER 25 ❧
FILL YOUR DAY WITH SHORT AND
ARDENT PRAYER

JULY 25, 2005

"Dear Children! Also today, I call you to fill your day with short and ardent prayer. When you pray, your hearts is open and God loves you with a special love and gives you special graces. Therefore, make good use of this time of grace and devote it to God more than ever up to now. Do novenas of fasting and renunciations so that Satan be far from you and grace be around you. I am near you and intercede before God for each of you. Thank you for having responded to my call."

❧ CHAPTER 26 ❧
FOLLOW ME; I WILL HELP YOU

JANUARY 2, 2007

"Dear children, in this holy time full of God's graces, and His love which sends me to you, I implore you not to have a heart of stone. May fasting and prayer be your weapon for drawing closer to Jesus, my Son, and coming to know Him. Follow me and my luminous example. I will help you. I am with you. Thank you!"

☙ CHAPTER 27 ❧
FORGIVENESS

JANUARY 25, 1996

"Dear Children! Today I invite you to decide for peace. Pray that God give you the true peace. Live peace in your hearts and you will understand, dear children, that peace is the gift of God. Dear children, without love you cannot live peace. The fruit of peace is love and the fruit of love is forgiveness. I am with you and I invite all of you, little children, that before all else forgive in the family and then you will be able to forgive others. Thank you for having responded to my call."

SEPTEMBER 2, 2009

"Dear children! Today, with a motherly heart, I call you to learn to forgive, completely and unconditionally. You suffer injustice, betrayals and prosecutions, but by that you are closer to and dearer to God. My children, pray for the gift of love. Only love forgives all, as my Son forgives – follow Him. I am among you and am praying that when you come before your Father you can say: 'Here I am Father, I followed your Son, I had love and forgave with the heart, because I believed in your judgment and trusted in you.' Thank you. "

JANUARY 2, 2010

"Dear children! Today I am calling you to, with complete trust and love, set out with me, because I desire to acquaint you with my Son. Do not be afraid, my children, I am here with you, I am next to you. I am showing you the way to forgive yourselves, to forgive others, and, with sincere repentance of heart, to kneel before the Father. Make everything die in you that hinders you from loving and saving - that you may be with Him and in Him. Decide for a new beginning, a beginning of sincere love of God Himself. Thank you."

SEPTEMBER 2, 2010

"Dear children, I am beside you because I desire to help you to overcome trials, which this time of purification puts before you. My children, one of those is not to forgive and not to ask for forgiveness. Every sin offends

Love and distances you from it – and Love is my Son. Therefore, my children, if you desire to walk with me towards the peace of God's love, you must learn to forgive and to ask for forgiveness. Thank you."

NOVEMBER 2, 2010
"Dear children! With motherly perseverance and love I am bringing you the light of life to destroy the darkness of death in you. Do not reject me, my children. Stop and look within yourselves and see how sinful you are. Be aware of your sins and pray for forgiveness. My children, you do not desire to accept that you are weak and little, but you can be strong and great by doing God's will. Give me your cleansed hearts that I may illuminate them with the light of life, my Son. Thank you."

ᕬ CHAPTER 28 ᕫ
GIVE GLORY TO GOD

AUGUST 25, 1999
"Dear children! Also today I call you to give glory to God the Creator in the colors of nature. He speaks to you also through the smallest flower about His beauty and the depth of love with which He has created you. Little children, may prayer flow from your hearts like fresh water from a spring. May the wheat fields speak to you about the mercy of God towards every creature. That is why, renew prayer of thanksgiving for everything He gives you. Thank you for having responded to my call."

ᕬ CHAPTER 29 ᕫ
GIVE JESUS ALL THAT IS ON YOUR HEART

MARCH 25, 2002
"Dear children! Today I call you to unite with Jesus in prayer. Open your heart to Him and give Him everything that is in it: joys, sorrows and illnesses. May this be a time of grace for you. Pray, little children, and may every moment belong to Jesus. I am with you and I intercede for you. Thank you for having responded to my call."

❧ CHAPTER 30 ❦

GIVE MARY ALL YOUR PROBLEMS

JUNE 20, 1985

"Dear children! For this Feast Day I wish to tell you to open your hearts to the Master of all hearts. Give me all your feelings and all your problems! I wish to comfort your in all your trials. I wish to fill you with peace, joy and love of God. Thank you for having responded to my call."

❧ CHAPTER 31 ❦

GIVE ME YOUR HEARTS

MAY 2, 2007

"Dear children! Today I come to you with a motherly desire for you to give me your hearts. My children, do this with complete trust and without fear. In your hearts, I will put my Son and His mercy. Then, my children, you will look at the world around you with different eyes. You will see your neighbor. You will feel his pain and suffering. You will not turn your head away from those who suffer, because my Son turns His head away from those who do so. Children, do not hesitate."

JUNE 2, 2007

"Dear children! Also in this difficult time God's love sends me to you. My children, do not be afraid, I am with you. With complete trust give me your hearts, that I may help you to recognize the signs of the time in which you live. I will help you to come to know the love of my Son. I will triumph through you. Thank you."

SEPTEMBER 2, 2007

"Dear children! In this time of God's signs, do not be afraid because I am with you. The great love of God sends me to lead you to salvation. Give me your simple hearts, purified by fasting and prayer. Only in the simplicity of your hearts is your salvation. I will be with you and will lead you. Thank you."

❧ CHAPTER 32 ❦
GOD DESIRES TO CONVERT THE ENTIRE WORLD

JUNE 25, 2007

"Dear children! Also today, with great joy in my heart, I call you to conversion. Little children, do not forget that you are all important in this great plan, which God leads through Medjugorje. God desires to convert the entire world and to call it to salvation and to the way towards Himself, who is the beginning and the end of every being. In a special way, little children, from the depth of my heart, I call you all to open yourselves to this great grace that God gives you through my presence here. I desire to thank each of you for the sacrifices and prayers. I am with you and I bless you all. Thank you for having responded to my call."

❧ CHAPTER 33 ❦
GOD DESIRES TO SAVE YOU ONE BY ONE

MARCH 25, 2003

"Dear children! Also today I call you to pray for peace. Pray with the heart, little children, and do not lose hope because God loves His creatures. He desires to save you, one by one, through my coming here. I call you to the way of holiness. Pray, and in prayer you are open to God's will; in this way, in everything you do, you realize God's plan in you and through you. Thank you for having responded to my call."

❧ CHAPTER 34 ❦
GOD IS CALLING YOU INDIVIDUALLY

APRIL 2, 2011

"Dear children; With motherly love I desire to open the heart of each of you and to teach you personal unity with the Father. To accept this, you must comprehend that you are important to God and that He is calling you individually. You must comprehend that your prayer is a conversation of a child with the Father; that love is the way by which you must set out - love for God and for your neighbor. That is, my children, the love that has no boundaries, that is the love that emanates from truth and goes to the end. Follow me, my children, so that also others, in recognizing the truth and love in you, may follow you. Thank you."

Once again Our Lady called us to pray for our shepherds (priests) and said: "They have a special place in my heart. They represent my Son."

❧ CHAPTER 35 ❦
GOD IS GREAT, GREAT ARE HIS WORKS

SEPTEMBER 2, 2006

"You know that we have been gathering for me to help you to come to know the love of God." She than spoke about the future and said: "I am gathering you under my motherly mantle to help you to come to know God's love and His greatness. My children, God is great. Great are His works. Do not deceive yourselves that you can do anything without Him. Not even to take a step, my children. Instead set out and witness His love! I am with you. Thank you."

❧ CHAPTER 36 ❧
GOD THE CREATOR

JULY 25, 2001

"Dear children! In this time of grace, I call you to come even closer to God through your personal prayer. Make good use of the time of rest and give your soul and your eyes rest in God. Find peace in nature and you will discover God the Creator Whom you will be able to give thanks to for all creatures; then you will find joy in your heart. Thank you for having responded to my call."

DECEMBER 25, 2007

"Dear children! With great joy I bring you the King of Peace for Him to bless you with His blessing. Adore Him and give time to the Creator for whom your heart yearns. Do not forget that you are passers-by on this earth and that things can give you small joys, while through my Son, eternal life is given to you. That is why I am with you, to lead you towards what your heart yearns for. Thank you for having responded to my call."

JULY 25, 2008

"Dear children! At this time when you are thinking of physical rest, I call you to conversion. Pray and work so that your heart yearns for God the Creator who is the true rest of your soul and your body. May He reveal His face to you and may He give you His peace. I am with you and intercede before God for each of you. Thank you for having responded to my call."

FEBRUARY 25, 2010

"Dear children! In this time of grace, when nature also prepares to give the most beautiful colors of the year, I call you, little children, to open your hearts to God the Creator for Him to transform and mold you in His image, so that all the good which has fallen asleep in your hearts may awaken to a new life and a longing towards eternity. Thank you for having responded to my call."

❧ CHAPTER 37 ◈
GOD THE FATHER

NOVEMBER 2, 2009

"Dear children! Also today I am among you to point you to the way that will help you to come to know God's love, the love of God Who permitted you to call Him Father and to perceive Him as Father. I ask of you to sincerely look into your hearts and to see how much you love Him. Is He the last to be loved? Surrounded by material goods, how many times have you betrayed, denied and forgotten Him? My children, do not deceive yourselves with worldly goods. Think of your soul because it is more important than the body, cleanse it. Invoke the Father, He is waiting for you. Come back to Him. I am with you because He, in His mercy, sends me. Thank you."

❧ CHAPTER 38 ◈
GOD WORKING THROUGH US

MARCH 6, 1986

"Dear children! Today I call you to open yourselves more to God, so that He can work through you. The more you open yourselves, the more you receive the fruits. I wish to call you again to prayer. Thank you for having responded to my call."

DECEMBER 25, 2000 (ANNUAL APPARITION TO JAKOV)

"Dear children! Today when Jesus is born and by His birth brings immeasurable joy, love and peace, I call you, in a special way to say your yes to Jesus. Open your hearts so that Jesus enters into them, comes to dwell in them and starts to work through you. Only in this way will you be able to comprehend the true beauty of God's love, joy and peace. Dear children, rejoice in the birth of Jesus and pray for all those hearts that have not opened to Jesus so that Jesus may enter into each of their hearts and may start working through them, so that every person would be an example of a true person through whom God works."

❧ CHAPTER 39 ❧
GOD'S BLESSING

APRIL 10, 1986

"Dear children! I desire to call you to grow in love. A flower is not able to grow normally without water. So also you, dear children, are not able to grow without God's blessing. From day to day you need to seek His blessing so you will grow normally and perform all your actions in union with God. Thank you for having responded to my call."

JUNE 25, 1987

"Dear children! Today I thank you and I want to invite you all to God's peace. I want each one of you to experience in your heart that peace which God gives. I want to bless you all today. I am blessing you with God's blessing and I beseech you, dear children, to follow and to live my way. I love you, dear children, and so not even counting the number of times, I go on calling you and I thank you for all that you are doing for my intentions. I beg you, help me to present you to God and to save you. Thank you for having responded to my call."

DECEMBER 25, 2006

"Dear children! Also today I bring you the newborn Jesus in my arms. He who is the King of Heaven and earth, He is your peace. Little children, no one can give you peace as He who is the King of Peace. Therefore, adore Him in your hearts, choose Him and you will have joy in Him. He will bless you with His blessing of peace. Thank you for having responded to my call."

DECEMBER 25, 2007

"Dear children! With great joy I bring you the King of Peace for Him to bless you with His blessing. Adore Him and give time to the Creator for whom your heart yearns. Do not forget that you are passers-by on this earth and that things can give you small joys, while through my Son, eternal life is given to you. That is why I am with you, to lead you towards what your heart yearns for. Thank you for having responded to my call."

❧ CHAPTER 40 ❧
GOD'S LOVE WILL BE GIVEN TO YOU AS A GIFT

DECEMBER 2, 2011
"Dear children, As a mother I am with you so that with my love, prayer and example I may help you to become a seed of the future, a seed that will grow into a firm tree and spread it's branches throughout the world. For you to become a seed of the future, a seed of love, implore the Father to forgive you your omissions up to now. My children, only a pure heart, unburdened by sin, can open itself and only honest eyes can see the way by which I desire to lead you. When you become aware of this, you will become aware of the love of God - it will be given (as a gift) to you. Then you will give it (as a gift) to others as a seed of love. Thank you."

❧ CHAPTER 41 ❧
GOD'S PLAN

SEPTEMBER 27, 1984
"Dear children! You have helped me along by your prayers to realize my plans. Keep on praying that my plans be completely fulfilled. I request the families of the parish to pray the family Rosary. Thank you for having responded to my call."

JANUARY 9, 1986
"Dear children! I call you by your prayers to help Jesus along in the fulfillment of all the plans which He is forming here. And offer your sacrifices to Jesus in order that everything is fulfilled the way He has

planned it and that Satan can accomplish nothing. Thank you for having responded to my call."

JANUARY 30, 1986

"Dear children! Today I call you all to pray that God's plans for us may be realized and also everything that God desires through you! Help others to be converted, especially those who are coming to Medjugorje. Dear children, do not allow Satan to get control of your hearts, so you would be an image of Satan and not of me. I call you to pray for how you might be witnesses of my presence. Without you, God cannot bring to reality that which He desires. God has given a free will to everyone, and it's in your control. Thank you for having responded to my call."

JANUARY 25, 1987

"Dear children! Behold, also today I want to call you to start living a new life as of today. Dear children, I want you to comprehend that God has chosen each one of you, in order to use you in His great plan for the salvation of mankind. You are not able to comprehend how great your role is in God's design. Therefore, dear children, pray so that in prayer you may be able to comprehend what God's plan is in your regard. I am with you in order that you may be able to bring it about in all its fullness. Thank you for having responded to my call."

APRIL 25, 1987

"Dear children! Today also I am calling you to prayer. You know, dear children, that God grants special graces in prayer. Therefore, seek and pray in order that you may be able to comprehend all that I am giving here. I call you, dear children, to prayer with the heart. You know that without prayer you cannot comprehend all that God is planning through each one of you. Therefore, pray! I desire that through each one of you God's plan may be fulfilled, that all which God has planted in your heart may keep on growing. So pray that God's blessing may protect each one of you from all the evil that is threatening you. I bless you, dear children. Thank you for having responded to my call."

SEPTEMBER 25, 1992

"Dear children! Today again I would like to say to you that I am with you also in these troubled days during which Satan wishes to destroy all that my Son Jesus and I are building. He desires especially to destroy your souls. He wants to take you away as far as possible from the Christian life and from the commandments that the Church calls you to live. Satan wishes to destroy everything that is holy in you and around you. This is why, little children, pray, pray, pray to be able to grasp all that God is giving you through my coming. Thank you for having responded to my call."

DECEMBER 25, 1992

"Dear children! I desire to place all of you under my mantle and protect you from all satanic attacks. Today is a day of peace, but in the whole world there is a great lack of peace. That is why I call you all to build a new world of peace with me through prayer. This I cannot do without you, and this is why I call all of you with my motherly love and God will do the rest. So, open yourselves to God's plan and to His designs to be able to cooperate with Him for peace and for everything that is good. Do not forget that your life does not belong to you, but is a gift with which you must bring joy to others and lead them to eternal life. May the tenderness of the little Jesus always accompany you. Thank you for having responded to my call."

JUNE 25, 2007

"Dear children! Also today, with great joy in my heart, I call you to conversion. Little children, do not forget that you are all important in this great plan, which God leads through Medjugorje. God desires to convert the entire world and to call it to salvation and to the way towards Himself, who is the beginning and the end of every being. In a special way, little children, from the depth of my heart, I call you all to open yourselves to this great grace that God gives you through my presence here. I desire to thank each of you for the sacrifices and prayers. I am with you and I bless you all. Thank you for having responded to my call."

FEBRUARY 25, 2009

"Dear children! In this time of renunciation, prayer and penance, I call you anew: go and confess your sins so that grace may open your hearts, and permit it to change you. Convert little children, open yourselves to God and to His plan for each of you. Thank you for having responded to my call."

JUNE 2, 2011

"Dear children! As I call you to prayer for those who have not come to know the love of God, if you were to look into your hearts you would comprehend that I am speaking about many of you. With an open heart, sincerely ask yourselves if you want the living God or do you want to eliminate Him and live as you want. Look around you, my children, and see where the world is going, the world that thinks of doing everything without the Father, and which wanders in the darkness of temptation. I am offering to you the light of the Truth and the Holy Spirit. According to God's plan I am with you to help you to have my Son, His Cross and Resurrection, triumph in your hearts. As a mother, I desire and pray for your unity with my Son and His works. I am with you; you decide. Thank you."

❧ CHAPTER 42 ❧
GROW IN GOD'S LOVE

MARCH 2, 2006

No message but Gospa exclaims, "God is love, God is love, God is love!"

APRIL 25, 2008

"Dear children! Also today, I call all of you to grow in God's love as a flower which feels the warm rays of spring. In this way, also you, little children, grow in God's love and carry it to all those who are far from God. Seek God's will and do good to those whom God has put on your way, and be light and joy. Thank you for having responded to my call."

❧ CHAPTER 43 ❧
HE GAVE HIS LIFE FOR YOU

SEPTEMBER 25, 2007
"Dear children! Also today I call all of you for your hearts to blaze with more ardent love for the Crucified, and do not forget that, out of love for you, He gave His life so that you may be saved. Little children, meditate and pray that your heart may be open to God's love. Thank you for having responded to my call."

❧ CHAPTER 44 ❧
HEAL OUR WOUNDS

MARCH 25, 1997
"Dear children! Today, in a special way, I invite you to take the cross in the hands and to meditate on the wounds of Jesus. Ask of Jesus to heal your wounds, which you, dear children, during your life sustained because of your sins or the sins of your parents. Only in this way, dear children, you will understand that the world is in need of healing of faith in God the Creator. By Jesus' passion and death on the cross, you will understand that only through prayer you, too, can become true apostles of faith; when, in simplicity and prayer, you live faith which is a gift. Thank you for having responded to my call."

❧ CHAPTER 45 ❧
HELP YOUR NEIGHBOR DISCOVER FAITH

OCTOBER 2, 2008
"Dear children; Again I call you to faith. My motherly heart desires for your heart to be open, so that it could say to your heart: believe. My children, only faith will give you strength in life's trials. It will renew your soul

and open the ways of hope. I am with you. I gather you around me because I desire to help you, so that you can help your neighbors to discover faith, which is the only joy and happiness of life. Thank you."

❧ CHAPTER 46 ❧
HOLINESS

OCTOBER 24, 1985

"Dear children! From day to day I wish to clothe you in holiness, goodness, obedience and God's love, so that from day to day you become more beautiful and more prepared for your Master. Dear children, listen to and live my messages. I wish to guide you. Thank you for having responded to my call."

JULY 10, 1986

"Dear children! Today I am calling you to holiness. Without holiness you cannot live. Therefore, with love overcome every sin and with love overcome all the difficulties which are coming to you. Dear children, I beseech you to live love within yourselves. Thank you for having responded to my call."

JULY 24, 1986

"Dear children! I rejoice because of all of you who are on the way of holiness and I beseech you, by your own testimony help those who do not know how to live in holiness. Therefore, dear children, let your family be a place where holiness is birthed. Help everyone to live in holiness, but especially your own family. Thank you for having responded to my call."

OCTOBER 9, 1986

"Dear children! You know that I desire to lead you on the way of holiness, but I do not want to compel you to be saints by force. I desire that each of you by your own little self-denials help yourself and me so I can lead you from day to day closer to holiness. Therefore, dear children, I do not desire to force you to observe the messages. But rather this long time that I am with you is a sign that I love you immeasurably and what I desire of each individual is to become holy.   Thank you for having responded to my call."

NOVEMBER 13, 1986

"Dear children! Today again I am calling you to pray with your whole heart and day by day to change your life. Especially, dear children, I am calling that by your prayers and sacrifices you begin to live in holiness, because I desire that each one of you who has been to this fountain of grace will come to Paradise with the special gift which you shall give me, and that is holiness. Therefore, dear children, pray and daily change your life in order to become fully holy. I shall always be close to you. Thank you for having responded to my call."

JANUARY 1, 1987

"Dear children! Today I wish to call on all of you that in the New Year you live the messages which I am giving you. Dear children, you know that for your sake I have remained a long time so I might teach you how to make progress on the way of holiness. Therefore, dear children, pray without ceasing and live the messages which I am giving you for I am doing it with great love toward God and toward you. Thank you for having responded to my call."

MAY 25, 1987

"Dear children! I am calling everyone of you to start living in God's love. Dear children, you are ready to commit sin, and to put yourselves in the hand of Satan without reflecting. I call on each one of you to consciously decide for God and against Satan. I am your Mother and, therefore, I want to lead you all to perfect holiness. I want each one of you to be happy here on earth and to be with me in Heaven. That is, dear children, the purpose of my coming here and it's my desire. Thank you for having responded to my call."

JULY 25, 1987

"Dear children! I beseech you to take up the way of holiness beginning today. I love you and, therefore, I want you to be holy. I do not want Satan to block you on that way. Dear children, pray and accept all that God is offering you on a way which is bitter. But at the same time, God will reveal every sweetness to whomever begins to go on that way, and He will gladly answer every call of God. Do not attribute importance to petty things. Long for Heaven. Thank you for having responded to my call."

AUGUST 25, 1987

"Dear children! Today also I am calling you all in order that each one of you decides to live my messages. God has permitted me also in this year, which the Church has dedicated to me, to be able to speak to you and to be able to spur you on to holiness. Dear children, seek from God the graces which He is giving you through me. I am ready to intercede with God for all that you seek so that your holiness may be complete. Therefore, dear children, do not forget to seek, because God has permitted me to obtain graces for you. Thank you for having responded to my call."

SEPTEMBER 25, 1987

"Dear children! Today also I want to call you all to prayer. Let prayer be your life. Dear children, dedicate your time only to Jesus and He will give you everything that you are seeking. He will reveal Himself to you in fullness. Dear children, Satan is strong and is waiting to test each one of you. Pray, and that way he will neither be able to injure you nor block you on the way of holiness. Dear children, through prayer grow all the more toward God from day to day. Thank you for having responded to my call."

APRIL 25, 1988

"Dear children! God wants to make you holy. Therefore, through me He is inviting you to complete surrender. Let holy mass be your life. Understand that the church is God's palace, the place in which I gather you and want to show you the way to God. Come and pray. Neither look at others nor slander them, but rather, let your life be a testimony on the way of holiness. Churches deserve respect and are set apart as holy because God, who became man, dwells in them day and night. Therefore, little children, believe and pray that the Father increase your faith, and then ask for whatever you need. I am with you and I am rejoicing because of your conversion and I am protecting you with my motherly mantle. Thank you for having responded to my call."

SEPTEMBER 25, 1988

"Dear children! Today I am inviting all of you, without exception, to the way of holiness in your life. God gave you the grace, the gift of holiness. Pray that you may, more and more, comprehend it, and in that way, you will be able, by your life, to bear witness for God. Dear children, I am blessing you and I intercede to God for you so that your way and your witness may be a complete one and a joy for God. Thank you for having responded to my call."

JANUARY 25, 1989

"Dear children! Today I am calling you to the way of holiness. Pray that you may comprehend the beauty and the greatness of this way where God reveals himself to you in a special way. Pray that you may be open to everything that God does through you that in your life you may be enabled to give thanks to God and to rejoice over everything that He does through each individual. I give you my blessing. Thank you for having responded to my call."

JUNE 25, 1991

"Dear children! Today on this great day which you have given to me, I desire to bless all of you and to say: these days while I am with you are days of grace. I desire to teach you and help you to walk the way of holiness. There are many people who do not desire to understand my messages and to accept with seriousness what I am saying. But you I therefore call and ask that by your lives and by your daily living you witness my presence. If you pray, God will help you to discover the true reason for my coming. Therefore, little children, pray and read the Sacred Scriptures so that through my coming you discover the message in Sacred Scripture for you. Thank you for having responded to my call."

APRIL 25, 1994

"Dear children! Today I invite you to decide to pray according to my intention. Little children, I invite each one of you to help my plan to be realized through this parish. Now I invite you in a special way, little children, to decide to go along the way of holiness. Only this way will you be close to me. I love you and I desire to conduct you all with me to

Paradise. But, if you do not pray and if you are not humble and obedient to the messages which I am giving you, I cannot help you. Thank you for having responded to my call."

MARCH 25, 2001

"Dear children! Also today I call you to open yourselves to prayer. Little children, you live in a time in which God gives great graces but you do not know how to make good use of them. You are concerned about everything else, but the least for the soul and spiritual life. Awaken from the tired sleep of your soul and say yes to God with all your strength. Decide for conversion and holiness. I am with you, little children, and I call you to perfection of your soul and of everything you do. Thank you for having responded to my call."

AUGUST 25, 2001

"Dear children! Today I call all of you to decide for holiness. May for you, little children, always in your thoughts and in each situation holiness be in the first place, in work and in speech. In this way, you will also put it into practice; little by little, step by step, prayer and a decision for holiness will enter into your family. Be real with yourselves and do not bind yourselves to material things but to God. And do not forget, little children, that your life is as passing as a flower. Thank you for having responded to my call."

DECEMBER 2, 2006

"Dear children, in this joyful time of expectation of my Son, I desire that all the days of your earthly life may be a joyful expectation of my Son. I am calling you to holiness. I call you to be my apostles of holiness so that, through you, the Good News may illuminate all those whom you will meet. Fast and pray, and I will be with you. Thank you!"

❧ CHAPTER 47 ❧
HOLY SPIRIT

JUNE 2, 1984 (SATURDAY)

"Dear children! Tonight I wish to tell you during the days of this novena to pray for the outpouring of the Holy Spirit on your families and on your parish. Pray, and you shall not regret it. God will give you gifts by which you will glorify Him till the end of your life on this earth. Thank you for having responded to my call."

NOVEMBER 8, 1984

"Dear children! You are not conscious of the messages which God is sending you through me. He is giving you great graces and you do not comprehend them. Pray to the Holy Spirit for enlightenment. If you only knew how great are the graces God is granting you, you would be praying without ceasing. Thank you for having responded to my call."

MAY 9, 1985

"Dear children! No, you do not know how many graces God is giving you. You do not want to move ahead during these days when the Holy Spirit is working in a special way. Your hearts are turned toward the things of earth and they preoccupy you. Turn your hearts toward prayer and seek the Holy Spirit to be poured out on you. Thank you for having responded to my call."

MAY 16, 1985

"Dear children! I am calling you to a more active prayer and attendance at Holy Mass. I wish your Mass to be an experience of God. I wish especially to say to the young people: be open to the Holy Spirit because God wishes to draw you to Himself in these days when Satan is at work. Thank you for having responded to my call."

MAY 23, 1985

"Dear children! These days I call you especially to open your hearts to the Holy Spirit. Especially during these days the Holy Spirit is working through you. Open your hearts and surrender your life to Jesus so that He works through your hearts and strengthens you in faith. Thank you for having responded to my call."

APRIL 17, 1986

"Dear children! You are absorbed with material things, but in the material you lose everything that God wishes to give you. I call you, dear children, to pray for the gifts of the Holy Spirit which are necessary for you now in order to be able to give witness to my presence here and to all that I am giving you. Dear children, let go to me so I can lead you completely. Don't be absorbed with material things. Thank you for having responded to my call."

MAY 25, 1993

"Dear children! Today I invite you to open yourselves to God by means of prayer so the Holy Spirit may begin to work miracles in you and through you. I am with you and I intercede before God for each one of you because, dear children, each one of you is important in my plan of salvation. I invite you to be carriers of good and peace. God can give you peace only if you convert and pray. Therefore, my dear little children, pray, pray, pray and do that which the Holy Spirit inspires you. Thank you for having responded to my call."

MAY 25, 1998

"Dear children! Today I call you, through prayer and sacrifice, to prepare yourselves for the coming of the Holy Spirit. Little children, this is a time of grace and so, again, I call you to decide for God the Creator. Allow Him to transform and change you. May your heart be prepared to listen to, and live, everything which the Holy Spirit has in His plan for each of you. Little children, allow the Holy Spirit to lead you on the way of truth and salvation towards eternal life. Thank you for having responded to my call."

MAY 25, 2000

"Dear children! I rejoice with you and in this time of grace I call you to spiritual renewal. Pray, little children, that the Holy Spirit may come to dwell in you in fullness, so that you may be able to witness in joy to all those who are far from faith. Especially, little children, pray for the gifts of the Holy Spirit so that in the spirit of love, every day and in each situation, you may be closer to your fellow-man; and that in wisdom and love you may overcome every difficulty. I am with you and I intercede for each of you before Jesus. Thank you for having responded to my call."

APRIL 25, 2004

"Dear children! Also today, I call you to live my messages even more strongly in humility and love so that the Holy Spirit may fill you with His grace and strength. Only in this way will you be witnesses of peace and forgiveness. Thank you for having responded to my call."

JULY 25, 2006

"Dear children! At this time, do not only think of rest for your body but, little children, seek time also for the soul. In silence may the Holy Spirit speak to you and permit Him to convert and change you. I am with you and before God I intercede for each of you. Thank you for having responded to my call."

NOVEMBER 2, 2007

"Dear children, today I call you to open your heart to the Holy Spirit and to permit Him to transform you. My children, God is the immeasurable good and therefore, as a mother, I implore you to pray, pray, pray, to fast and to hope that it is possible to attain that good, because love is born of that good. The Holy Spirit will reinforce that good in you and you will be able to call God your Father. Through this exalted love, you will sincerely come to love all people and, through God, consider them brothers and sisters. Thank you."

MAY 25, 2009

"Dear children! In this time, I call you all to pray for the coming of the Holy Spirit upon every baptized creature, so that the Holy Spirit may renew you all and lead you on the way of witnessing your faith – you and all those who are far from God and His love. I am with you and intercede for you before the Most High. Thank you for having responded to my call."

JANUARY 25, 2011

"Dear children! Also today I am with you and I am looking at you and blessing you, and I am not losing hope that this world will change for the good and that peace will reign in the hearts of men. Joy will begin to reign in the world because you have opened yourselves to my call and to God's love. The Holy Spirit is changing a multitude of those who have said 'yes'. Therefore I desire to say to you: thank you for having responded to my call."

❧ CHAPTER 48 ❧
I AM HERE TO LEAD YOU AND CAUTION YOU

AUGUST 25, 2009

"Dear children; I am coming, with my motherly love, to point out the way by which you are to set out, in order that you may be all the more like my Son; and by that, closer to and more pleasing to God. Do not refuse my love. Do not renounce salvation and eternal life for the sake of transience and frivolity of this life. I am among you to lead you and, as a mother, to caution you. Come with me."

❧ CHAPTER 49 ❧
I AM THE QUEEN OF PEACE;
PLEASE PERMIT ME TO LEAD YOU

AUGUST 2, 2006

"Dear children, In these peaceless times I am coming to you to show you the way to peace. I love with an immeasurable love and I desire for you to love each other and to see in everyone my Son – the immeasurable love. The way to peace leads solely and only through love. Give your hand to me, your mother, and permit me to lead you. I am the Queen of Peace. Thank you."

❧ CHAPTER 50 ❧
I AM YOUR MOTHER

NOVEMBER 29, 1984

"Dear children! No, you don't know how to love and you don't know how to listen with love to the words I am saying to you. Be conscious, my beloved, that I am your Mother and I have come on earth to teach you to listen out of love, to pray out of love and not compelled by the fact that you are carrying a cross. By means of the cross God is glorified through every person. Thank you for having responded to my call."

JANUARY 31, 1985

"Dear children! Today I wish to tell you to open your hearts to God like the spring flowers which crave for the sun. I am your Mother and I always want you to be closer to the Father and that He will always give abundant gifts to your hearts. Thank you for having responded to my call."

NOVEMBER 14, 1985

"Dear children! I, your Mother, love you and wish to urge you to prayer. I am tireless, dear children, and I am calling you even then, when you are far away from my heart. I am a Mother, and even though I feel pain for each one who goes astray, I forgive easily and am happy for every child who returns to me. Thank you for having responded to my call."

❧ CHAPTER 51 ❧
I DESIRE TO ILLUMINATE YOUR SOULS
WITH A NEW LIGHT

JUNE 2, 2008

"Dear children, I am with you by the grace of God, to make you great - great in faith and love - all of you! You whose heart has been hard as a stone by sin and guilt, but you devout souls, I desire to illuminate with a new light. Pray that my prayer may meet open hearts that I may be able to illuminate them with the strength of faith and open the ways of love and hope. Be persevering. I will be with you."

↣ CHAPTER 52 ↢
I DESIRE TO INSPIRE YOU ALL

JANUARY 25, 2010

"Dear children! May this time be a time of personal prayer for you, so that the seed of faith may grow in your hearts; and may it grow into a joyful witness to others. I am with you and I desire to inspire you all: grow and rejoice in the Lord Who has created you. Thank you for having responded to my call."

↣ CHAPTER 53 ↢
I NEED YOU

JULY 2, 2009

"Dear children! I am calling you because I need you. I need hearts ready for immeasurable love – hearts that are not burdened by vanity – hearts that are ready to love as my Son loved – that are ready to sacrifice themselves as my Son sacrificed himself. I need you. In order to come with me, forgive yourselves, forgive others and adore my Son. Adore him also for those who have not come to know him, those who do not love him. Therefore, I need you; therefore, I call you. Thank you."

↣ CHAPTER 54 ↢
I OFFER YOU THE KINGDOM OF GOD

AUGUST 2, 2010

"Dear children! Today I call you, together with me, to begin to build the Kingdom of Heaven in your hearts; that you may forget that what is personal and – led by the example of my Son – think of what is of God. What does He desire of you? Do not permit Satan to open the paths of earthly happiness, the paths without my Son. My children, they are false and last a short while. My Son exists. I offer you eternal happiness and peace and unity with my Son, with God; I offer you the Kingdom of God. Thank you."

❧ CHAPTER 55 ❦
I WILL TEACH YOU LOVE

MARCH 2, 2010

"Dear children! In this special time of your effort to be all the closer to my Son, to His suffering, but also to the love with which He bore it, I desire to tell you that I am with you. I will help you to triumph over errors and temptations with my grace. I will teach you love, love which wipes away all sins and makes you perfect, love which gives you the peace of my Son now and forever. Peace with you and in you, because I am the Queen of Peace. Thank you."

❧ CHAPTER 56 ❦
IN YOUR TIME THE GREAT GRACE OF GOD
DESCENDED ON EARTH

APRIL 2, 2008

"Dear children! Also today, as I am with you in the great love of God, I desire to ask you: Are you with me? Is your heart open for me? Do you permit me to purify and prepare it for my Son? My children, you are chosen because, in your time, the great grace of God descended on earth. Do not hesitate to accept it. Thank you."

❧ CHAPTER 57 ❦
JESUS

DECEMBER 12, 1985

"Dear children! For Christmas my invitation is that together we glorify Jesus. I present Him to you in a special way on that day and my invitation to you is that on that day we glorify Jesus and His nativity. Dear children, on that day pray still more and think more about Jesus. Thank you for having responded to my call."

MARCH 18, 2000 (ANNUAL APPARITION TO MIRJANA SOLDO)

"Dear children! Do not seek peace and happiness in vain, in the wrong places and in wrong things. Do not permit your hearts to become hard by loving vanity. Invoke the name of my Son. Receive Him in your heart. Only in the name of my Son will you experience true happiness and true peace in your heart. Only in this way will you come to know the love of God and spread it further. I am calling you to be my apostles."

DECEMBER 25, 2005

"Dear children ! Also today, in my arms I bring you little Jesus, the King of Peace, to bless you with His peace. Little children, in a special way today I call you to be my carriers of peace in this peaceless world. God will bless you. Little children, do not forget that I am your mother. I bless you all with a special blessing, with little Jesus in my arms. Thank you for having responded to my call."

DECEMBER 25, 2006

"Dear children! Also today I bring you the newborn Jesus in my arms. He who is the King of Heaven and earth, He is your peace. Little children, no one can give you peace as He who is the King of Peace. Therefore, adore Him in your hearts, choose Him and you will have joy in Him. He will bless you with His blessing of peace. Thank you for having responded to my call."

DECEMBER 25, 2008

"Dear children! You are running, working, gathering – but without blessing. You are not praying! Today I call you to stop in front of the manger and to meditate on Jesus, Whom I give to you today also, to bless you and to help you to comprehend that, without Him, you have no future. Therefore, little children, surrender your lives into the hands of Jesus, for Him to lead you and protect you from every evil. Thank you for having responded to my call."

❧ CHAPTER 58 ❦
LAMENT FOR MESSAGES

AUGUST 25, 1997
"Dear children! God gives me this time as a gift to you, so that I may instruct and lead you on the path of salvation. Dear children, now you do not comprehend this grace, but soon a time will come when you will lament for these messages. That is why, little children, live all of the words which I have given you through this time of grace and renew prayer, until prayer becomes a joy for you. Especially, I call all those who have consecrated themselves to my Immaculate Heart to become an example to others. I call all priests and religious brothers and sisters to pray the Rosary and to teach others to pray. The Rosary, little children, is especially dear to me. Through the Rosary open your heart to me and I am able to help you. Thank you for having responded to my call."

❧ CHAPTER 59 ❦
LEAVE SIN

APRIL 25, 1997
"Dear children! Today I call you to have your life be connected with God the Creator, because only in this way will your life have meaning and you will comprehend that God is love. God sends me to you out of love, that I may help you to comprehend that without Him there is no future or joy and, above all, there is no eternal salvation. Little children, I call you to leave sin

and to accept prayer at all times, that you may in prayer come to know the meaning of your life. God gives Himself to him who seeks Him. Thank you for having responded to my call."

JULY 25, 2000

"Dear children! Do not forget that you are here on earth on the way to eternity and that your home is in Heaven. That is why, little children, be open to God's love and leave egoism and sin. May your joy be only in discovering God in daily prayer. That is why, make good use of this time and pray, pray, pray; and God is near to you in prayer and through prayer. Thank you for having responded to my call."

JANUARY 25, 2002

"Dear children! At this time while you are still looking back to the past year I call you, little children, to look deeply into your heart and to decide to be closer to God and to prayer. Little children, you are still attached to earthly things and little to spiritual life. May my call today also be an encouragement to you to decide for God and for daily conversion. You cannot be converted, little children, if you do not abandon sins and do not decide for love towards God and neighbor. Thank you for having responded to my call."

SEPTEMBER 25, 2005

"Dear children! In love I call you: convert, even though you are far from my heart. Do not forget, I am your mother and I feel pain for each one who is far from my heart; but I do not leave you alone. I believe you can leave the way of sin and decide for holiness. Thank you for having responded to my call."

JANUARY 25, 2008

"Dear children! With the time of Lent, you are approaching a time of grace. Your heart is like ploughed soil and it is ready to receive the fruit which will grow into what is good. You, little children, are free to choose good or evil. Therefore, I call you to pray and fast. Plant joy and the fruit of joy will grow in your hearts for your good, and others will see it and receive it through your life. Renounce sin and choose eternal life. I am with you and intercede for you before my Son. Thank you for having responded to my call."

OCTOBER 2, 2009

"Dear Children! As I look at you, my heart seizes with pain. Where are you going my children? Have you sunk so deeply into sin that you do not know how to stop yourselves? You justify yourselves with sin and live according to it. Kneel down beneath the Cross and look at my Son. He conquered sin and died so that you, my children, may live. Permit me to help you not to die but to live with my Son forever. Thank you!"

MAY 25, 2011

"Dear children! My prayer today is for all of you who seek the grace of conversion. You knock on the door of my heart, but without hope and prayer, in sin, and without the Sacrament of Reconciliation with God. Leave sin and decide, little children, for holiness. Only in this way can I help you, hear your prayers and seek intercession before the Most High. Thank you for having responded to my call."

&ed CHAPTER 60 &S
LIFE OR DEATH; CHOOSE LIFE

JULY 2, 2006

"Dear children, God created you with free will to comprehend and to choose: Life or Death. I as a mother, with motherly love, desire to help you to comprehend and choose life. My children, do not deceive yourselves with false peace and false joy. Permit me, my children, to show you the true way, the way that leads to life –my Son. Thank you!"

❧ CHAPTER 61 ❦
LIVE MY MESSAGES

NOVEMBER 22, 1984

"Dear children! These days live all the main messages and keep rooting them in your hearts till Thursday. Thank you for having responded to my call."

SEPTEMBER 19, 1985 / SEPTEMBER 20, 1985

"Dear children! Today I invite you to live in humility all the messages which I am giving you. Do not become arrogant living the messages and saying 'I am living the messages.' If you shall bear and live the messages in your heart, everyone will feel it so that words, which serve those who do not obey, will not be necessary. For you, dear children, it is necessary to live and witness by your lives. Thank you for having responded to my call."

OCTOBER 10, 1985

"Dear children! I wish also today to call you to live the messages in the parish. Especially I wish to call the youth of the parish, who are dear to me. Dear children, if you live the messages, you are living the seed of holiness. I, as the Mother, wish to call you all to holiness so that you can bestow it on others. You are a mirror to others! Thank you for having responded to my call."

JANUARY 16, 1986

"Dear children! Today also I am calling you to prayer. Your prayers are necessary to me so that God may be glorified through all of you. Dear children, I pray you, obey and live the Mother's invitation, because only out of love am I calling you in order that I might help you. Thank you for having responded to my call."

FEBRUARY 27, 1986

"Dear children! In humility live the messages which I am giving you. Thank you for having responded to my call."

JUNE 5, 1986

"Dear children! Today I am calling on you to decide whether or not you wish to live the messages which I am giving you. I wish you to be active in living and spreading the messages. Especially, dear children, I wish that you all be the reflection of Jesus, which will enlighten this unfaithful world walking in darkness. I wish all of you to be the light for everyone and that you give witness in the light. Dear children, you are not called to the darkness, but you are called to the light. Therefore, live the light with your own life. Thank you for having responded to my call."

JULY 17, 1986

"Dear children! Today I am calling you to reflect upon why I am with you this long. I am the Mediatrix between you and God. Therefore, dear children, I desire to call you to live always out of love all that which God desires of you. For that reason, dear children, in your own humility live all the messages which I am giving you. Thank you for having responded to my call."

OCTOBER 9, 1986

"Dear children! You know that I desire to lead you on the way of holiness, but I do not want to compel you to be saints by force. I desire that each of you by your own little self-denials help yourself and me so I can lead you from day to day closer to holiness. Therefore, dear children, I do not desire to force you to observe the messages. But rather this long time that I am with you is a sign that I love you immeasurably and what I desire of each individual is to become holy. Thank you for having responded to my call."

OCTOBER 30, 1986

"Dear children! Today again I desire to call you to take seriously and carry out the messages which I am giving you. Dear children, it is for your sake that I have stayed this long so I could help you to fulfill all the messages which I am giving you. Therefore, dear children, out of love for me carry out all the messages which I am giving you. Thank you for having responded to my call."

JANUARY 1, 1987

"Dear children! Today I wish to call on all of you that in the New Year you live the messages which I am giving you. Dear children, you know that for your sake I have remained a long time so I might teach you how to make progress on the way of holiness. Therefore, dear children, pray without ceasing and live the messages which I am giving you for I am doing it with great love toward God and toward you. Thank you for having responded to my call."

JANUARY 8, 1987

"Dear children! I desire to thank you for every response to the messages. Especially, dear children, thank you for all the sacrifices and prayers which you have presented to me. Dear children, I desire to keep on giving you still further messages, only not every Thursday, dear children, but on each 25th in the month. The time has come when what my Lord desired has been fulfilled. Now I will give you less messages, but I am still with you. Therefore, dear children, I beseech you, listen to my messages and live them, so I can guide you. Dear children, thank you for having responded to my call."

AUGUST 25, 1987

"Dear children! Today also I am calling you all in order that each one of you decides to live my messages. God has permitted me also in this year, which the Church has dedicated to me, to be able to speak to you and to be able to spur you on to holiness. Dear children, seek from God the graces which He is giving you through me. I am ready to intercede with God for all that you seek so that your holiness may be complete. Therefore, dear children, do not forget to seek, because God has permitted me to obtain graces for you. Thank you for having responded to my call."

JUNE 25, 1989

"Dear children! Today I am calling you to live the messages I have been giving you during the past eight years. This is the time of grace and I desire the grace of God be great for every single one of you. I am blessing you and I love you with a special love. Thank you for having responded to call."

DECEMBER 25, 1989

"Dear children! Today I bless you in a special way with my motherly blessing and I am interceding for you before God that He gives you the gift of conversion of the heart. For years I am calling you and exhorting you to a deep spiritual life in simplicity, but you are so cold. Therefore, little children, I ask you to accept and live the messages with seriousness, so that your soul will not be sad when I will no longer be with you, and when I will no longer lead you like insecure children in their first steps. Therefore, little children, every day read the messages that I have given you and transform them into life. I love you and therefore I am calling you all to the way of salvation with God. Thank you for having responded to my call."

APRIL 25, 1990

"Dear children! Today I invite you to accept with seriousness and to live the messages which I am giving you. I am with you and I desire, dear children, that each one of you be ever closer to my heart. Therefore, little children, pray and seek the will of God in your everyday life. I desire that each one of you discover the way of holiness and grow in it until eternity. I will pray for you and intercede for you before God that you understand the greatness of this gift which God is giving me that I can be with you. Thank you for having responded to my call."

AUGUST 25, 1990

"Dear children! I desire to invite you to take with seriousness and put into practice the messages which I am giving you. You know, little children, that I am with you and I desire to lead you along the same path to heaven, which is beautiful for those who discover it in prayer. Therefore, little children, do not forget that those messages which I am giving you have to be put into your everyday life in order that you might be able to say: "There, I have taken the messages and tried to live them." Dear children, I am protecting you before the heavenly Father by my own prayers. Thank you for having responded to my call."

MAY 25, 1991

"Dear Children! Today I invite all of you who have heard my message of peace to realize it with seriousness and with love in your life. There are many who think that they are doing a lot by talking about the messages, but do not live them. Dear children, I invite you to life and to change all the negative in you, so that it all turns into the positive and life. Dear children, I am with you and I desire to help each of you to live and by living, to witness the good news. I am here, dear children, to help you and to lead you to heaven, and in heaven is the joy through which you can already live heaven now. Thank you for having responded to my call!"

MARCH 25, 1992

"Dear children! Today as never before I invite you to live my messages and to put them into practice in your life. I have come to you to help you and, therefore, I invite you to change your life because you have taken a path of misery, a path of ruin. When I told you: convert, pray, fast, be reconciled, you took these messages superficially. You started to live them and then you stopped, because it was difficult for you. No, dear children, when something is good, you have to persevere in the good and not think: God does not see me, He is not listening, He is not helping. And so you have gone away from God and from me because of your miserable interest. I wanted to create of you an oasis of peace, love and goodness. God wanted you, with your love and with His help, to do miracles and, thus, give an example. Therefore, here is what I say to you: Satan is playing with you and with your souls and I cannot help you because you are far away from my heart. Therefore, pray, live my messages and then you will see the miracles of God's love in your everyday life. Thank you for having responded to my call."

OCTOBER 25, 1993

"Dear children! These years I have been calling you to pray, to live what I am telling you, but you are living my messages a little. You talk, but do not live, that is why little children, this war is lasting so long. I invite you to open yourselves to God and in your hearts to live with God, living the good and giving witness to my messages. I love you and wish to protect you from every evil, but you do not desire it. Dear children, I cannot help you if you do not live God's commandments, if you do not live the mass, if you do not give up sin. I invite you to be apostles of love and goodness. In this world of unrest give witness to God and God's love, and God will bless you and give you what you seek from Him. Thank you for having responded to my call."

MAY 25, 1994

"Dear children! I invite you all to have more trust in me and to live my messages more deeply. I am with you and I intercede before God for you but also I wait for your hearts to open up to my messages. Rejoice because God loves you and gives you the possibility to convert every day and to believe more in God the Creator. Thank you having responded to my call."

JUNE 25, 1994

"Dear children! Today I rejoice in my heart in seeing you all present here. I bless you and I call you all to decide to live my messages which I give you here. I desire, little children, to guide you all to Jesus because He is your salvation. Therefore, little children, the more you pray the more you will be mine and of my Son, Jesus. I bless you all with my motherly blessing and I thank you for having responded to my call."

FEBRUARY 25, 1996

"Dear children! Today I invite you to conversion. This is the most important message that I have given you here. Little children, I wish that each of you become a carrier of my messages. I invite you, little children, to live the messages that I have given you over these years. This time is a time of grace. Especially now, when the Church also is inviting you to prayer and conversion. I also, little children, invite you to live my messages that I have given you during the time since I appear here. Thank you for having responded to my call."

DECEMBER 25, 1996

"Dear children! Today I am with you in a special way, holding little Jesus in my lap and I invite you, little children, to open yourselves to His call. He calls you to joy. Little children, joyfully live the messages of the Gospel, which I am repeating in the time since I am with you. Little children, I am your Mother and I desire to reveal to you the God of love and the God of peace. I do not desire for your life to be in sadness but that it be realized in joy for eternity, according to the Gospel. Only in this way will your life have meaning. Thank you for having responded to my call."

OCTOBER 25, 1997

"Dear children! Also today I am with you and I call all of you to renew yourselves by living my messages. Little children, may prayer be life for you and may you be an example to others. Little children, I desire for you to become carriers of peace and of God's joy to today's world without peace. That is why, little children, pray, pray, pray! I am with you and I bless you with my motherly peace. Thank you for having responded to my call."

JUNE 25, 2002

"Dear children! Today I pray for you and with you that the Holy Spirit may help you and increase your faith, so that you may accept even more the messages that I am giving you here in this holy place. Little children, comprehend that this is a time of grace for each of you; and with me, little children, you are secure. I desire to lead you all on the way of holiness. Live my messages and put into life every word that I am giving you. May they be precious to you because they come from heaven. Thank you for having responded to my call."

JUNE 25, 2003

"Dear children! Also today, I call you with great joy to live my messages. I am with you and I thank you for putting into life what I am saying to you. I call you to renew my messages even more, with new enthusiasm and joy. May prayer be your daily practice. Thank you for having responded to my call."

MAY 25, 2005

"Dear children! Anew I call you to live my messages in humility. Especially witness them now when we are approaching the anniversary of my apparitions. Little children, be a sign to those who are far from God and His love. I am with you and bless you all with my motherly blessing. Thank you for having responded to my call."

JUNE 25, 2008

"Dear children! Also today, with great joy in my heart, I call you to follow me and to listen to my messages. Be joyful carriers of peace and love in this peaceless world. I am with you and I bless you all with my Son Jesus, the King of Peace. Thank you for having responded to my call."

JUNE 25, 2010

"Dear children! With joy, I call you all to live my messages with joy; only in this way, little children, will you be able to be closer to my Son. I desire to lead you all only to Him, and in Him you will find true peace and the joy of your heart. I bless you all and love you with immeasurable love. Thank you for having responded to my call."

❧ CHAPTER 62 ❧
LIVES OF SAINTS

OCTOBER 25, 1994

"Dear children! I am with you and I rejoice today because the Most High has granted me to be with you and to teach you and to guide you on the path of perfection. Little children, I wish you to be a beautiful bouquet of flowers which I wish to present to God for the day of All Saints. I invite you to open yourselves and to live, taking the saints as an example. Mother Church has chosen them, that they may be an impulse for your daily life. Thank you for having responded to my call!"

OCTOBER 25, 2004

"Dear children! This is a time of grace for the family and, therefore, I call you to renew prayer. May Jesus be in the heart of your family. In prayer, learn to love everything that is holy. Imitate the lives of saints so that they may be an incentive and teachers on the way of holiness. May every family become a witness of love in this world without prayer and peace. Thank you for having responded to my call."

SEPTEMBER 25, 2006

"Dear children! Also today I am with you and call all of you to complete conversion. Decide for God, little children, and you will find in God the peace your heart seeks. Imitate the lives of saints and may they be an example for you; and I will inspire you as long as the Almighty permits me to be with you. Thank you for having responded to my call."

JULY 25, 2007

"Dear children! Today, on the day of the Patron of your Parish, I call you to imitate the lives of the Saints. May they be, for you, an example and encouragement to a life of holiness. May prayer for you be like the air you breathe in and not a burden. Little children, God will reveal His love to you and you will experience the joy that you are my beloved. God will bless you and give you an abundance of grace. Thank you for having responded to my call."

OCTOBER 25, 2010

"Dear children! May this time be a time of prayer for you. My call, little children, desires to be for you a call to decide to follow the way of conversion; therefore, pray and seek the intercession of all the saints. May they be for you an example, an incentive and a joy towards eternal life. Thank you for having responded to my call."

☙ CHAPTER 63 ❧
LOVE (SACRIFICE)

JULY 4, 1985

"Dear children! I thank you for every sacrifice you have offered. And now I urge you to offer every sacrifice with love. I wish you, the helpless ones, to begin helping with confidence and the Lord will keep on giving to you in confidence. Thank you for having responded to my call."

MARCH 27, 1986

"Dear children! I wish to thank you for all the sacrifices and I invite you to the greatest sacrifice, the sacrifice of love. Without love, you are not able to accept either me or my Son. Without love, you cannot give an account of your experiences to others. Therefore, dear children, I call you to begin to live love within yourselves. Thank you for having responded to my call."

"Dear children! Today I wish to give you my own love. You do not know, dear children, how great my love is, and you do not know how to accept it. In various ways I wish to show it to you, but you, dear children, do not recognize it. You do not understand my words with your heart and neither are you able to comprehend my love. Dear children, accept me in your life and so you will be able to accept all I am saying to you and to which I am calling you. Thank you for having responded to my call."

"Dear children! Today my call to you is that in your life you live love toward God and neighbor. Without love, dear children, you can do nothing. Therefore, dear children, I am calling you to live in mutual love. Only in that way will you be able to love and accept both me and all those around you who are coming into your parish. Everyone will sense my love through you. Therefore, I beseech you, dear children, to start loving from today with an ardent love, the love with which I love you. Thank you for having responded to my call."

"Dear children! Hatred gives birth to dissensions and does not regard anyone or anything. I call you always to bring harmony and peace. Especially, dear children, in the place where you live, act with love. Let your only instrument always be love. By love turn everything into good which Satan desires to destroy and possess. Only that way shall you be completely mine and I shall be able to help you. Thank you for having responded to my call."

"Dear children! Today again I thank you for all that you have accomplished for me in these days. Especially, dear children, I thank you in the Name of Jesus for the sacrifices which you offered in this past week. Dear children, you are forgetting that I desire sacrifices from you so I can help you and drive Satan away from you. Therefore, I am calling you again to offer sacrifices with a special reverence toward God. Thank you for having responded to my call."

NOVEMBER 20, 1986

"Dear children! Today also I am calling you to live and follow with a special love all the messages which I am giving you. Dear children, God does not want you lukewarm and undecided, but that you totally surrender to Him. You know that I love you and that out of love I long for you. Therefore, dear children, you also decide for love so that you will long for and daily experience God's love. Dear children, decide for love so that love prevails in all of you, but not human love, rather God's love. Thank you for having responded to my call."

APRIL 25, 1993

"Dear children! Today I invite you all to awaken your hearts to love. Go into nature and look how nature is awakening and it will be a help to you to open your hearts to the love of God, the Creator. I desire you to awaken love in your families so that where there is unrest and hatred, love will reign and when there is love in your hearts then there is also prayer. And, dear children, do not forget that I am with you and I am helping you with my prayer that God may give you the strength to love. I bless and love you with my motherly love. Thank you for having responded to my call."

APRIL 25, 1995

"Dear children! Today I call you to love. Little children, without love you can neither live with God nor with brother. Therefore, I call all of you to open your hearts to the love of God that is so great and open to each one of you. God, out of love for man, has sent me among you to show you the path of salvation, the path of love. If you do not first love God, then you will neither be able to love neighbor nor the one you hate. Therefore, little children, pray and through prayer you will discover love. Thank you for having responded to my call."

NOVEMBER 25, 1995

"Dear Children! Today I invite you that each of you begin again to love, in the first place, God who saved and redeemed each of you, and then brothers and sisters in your proximity. Without love, little children, you cannot grow in holiness and cannot do good deeds. Therefore, little children, pray without ceasing that God reveals His love to you. I have invited all of you to unite yourselves with me and to love. Today I am with you and invite you to discover love in your hearts and in the families. For God to live in your hearts, you must love. Thank you for having responded to my call."

SEPTEMBER 25, 1997

"Dear children! Today I call you to comprehend that without love you cannot comprehend that God needs to be in the first place in your life. That is why, little children, I call you all to love, not with a human but with God's love. In this way, your life will be more beautiful and without an interest. You will comprehend that God gives Himself to you in the simplest way out of love. Little children, so that you may comprehend my words which I give you out of love, pray, pray, pray and you will be able to accept others with love and to forgive all who have done evil to you. Respond with prayer; prayer is a fruit of love towards God the Creator. Thank you for having responded to my call."

MARCH 25, 2005

"Dear children! Today I call you to love. Little children, love each other with God's love. At every moment, in joy and in sorrow, may love prevail and, in this way, love will begin to reign in your hearts. The risen Jesus will be with you and you will be His witnesses. I will rejoice with you and protect you with my motherly mantle. Especially, little children, I will watch your daily conversion with love. Thank you for having responded to my call."

MARCH 18, 2010

"Dear children! Today I call you to love with all your heart and with all your soul. Pray for the gift of love, because when the soul loves it calls my Son to itself. My Son does not refuse those who call Him and who desire to live according to Him. Pray for those who do not comprehend love, who do not understand what it means to love. Pray that God may be their Father and not their Judge. My children, you be my apostles, be my river of love. I need you. Thank you."

❧ CHAPTER 64 ❧
LOVE GOD AND LIVE HIS COMMANDMENTS

MAY 25, 2010

"Dear children! God gave you the grace to live and to defend all the good that is in you and around you, and to inspire others to be better and holier; but Satan, too, does not sleep and through modernism diverts you and leads you to his way. Therefore, little children, in the love for my Immaculate Heart, love God above everything and live His commandments. In this way, your life will have meaning and peace will rule on earth. Thank you for having responded to my call."

❧ CHAPTER 65 ❧
LOVE WORKS MIRACLES

SEPTEMBER 2, 2008

"Dear children, Today, with my motherly heart, I call you gathered around me to love your neighbor. My children, stop. Look in the eyes of your brother and see Jesus, my Son. If you see joy, rejoice with him. If there is pain in the eyes of your brother, with your tenderness and goodness, cast it away, because without love you are lost. Only love is effective; it works miracles. Love will give you unity in my Son and the victory of my heart. Therefore, my children, love."

&⤝ CHAPTER 66 ⤝&
LOVE YOUR NEIGHBOR

JUNE 6, 1985

"Dear children! During these days people from all nations will be coming into the parish. And now I am calling you to love: love first of all your own household members, and then you will be able to accept and love all who are coming. Thank you for having responded to my call."

NOVEMBER 7, 1985

"Dear children! I am calling you to the love of neighbor and love toward the one from whom evil comes to you. In that way with love you will be able to discern the intentions of hearts. Pray and love, dear children! By love you are able to do even that which you think is impossible. Thank you for having responded to my call."

DECEMBER 19, 1985

"Dear children! Today I wish to call you to love of neighbor. The more you will to love your neighbor, the more you shall experience Jesus especially on Christmas Day. God will bestow great gifts on you if you surrender yourselves to Him. I wish in a special way on Christmas Day to give mothers my own special motherly blessing, and Jesus will bless the rest with His own blessing. Thank you for having responded to my call."

JULY 2, 2008

"Dear children! With motherly love I desire to encourage you to love your neighbor. May my Son be the source of that love. He, who could have done everything by force, chose love and gave an example to you. Also today, through me, God expresses immeasurable goodness to you and, you children, are obliged to respond to it. With equal goodness and generosity behave towards the souls whom you meet. May your love convert them. In that way my Son and His love will resurrect in you. Thank you."

❧ CHAPTER 67 ❦
MARY'S HELP (HER HELP)

OCTOBER 25, 1984

"Dear children! Pray during this month. God allows me every day to help you with graces to defend yourselves against evil. This is my month. I want to give it to you. You just pray and God will give you the graces you are seeking. I will help along with it. Thank you for having responded to my call."

DECEMBER 4, 1986

"Dear children! Today I call you to prepare your hearts for these days when the Lord particularly desires to purify you from all the sins of your past. You, dear children, are not able by yourselves, therefore I am here to help you. You pray, dear children! Only that way shall you be able to recognize all the evil that is in you and surrender it to the Lord so the Lord may completely purify your hearts. Therefore, dear children, pray without ceasing and prepare your hearts in penance and fasting. Thank you for having responded to my call."

FEBRUARY 25, 1992

"Dear children! Today I invite you to draw still closer to God through prayer. Only that way will I be able to help you and to protect you from every attack of Satan. I am with you and I intercede for you with God, that He protect you. But I need your prayers and your - "Yes." You get lost easily in material and human things, and forget that God is your greatest friend. Therefore, my dear little children, draw close to God so He may protect you and guard you from every evil. Thank you for having responded to my call!"

APRIL 25, 2006

"Dear children! Also today I call you to have more trust in me and my Son. He has conquered by His death and resurrection and, through me, calls you to be a part of His joy. You do not see God, little children, but if you pray you will feel His nearness. I am with you and intercede before God for each of you. Thank you for having responded to my call."

MARCH 2, 2010

"Dear children! In this special time of your effort to be all the closer to my Son, to His suffering, but also to the love with which He bore it, I desire to tell you that I am with you. I will help you to triumph over errors and temptations with my grace. I will teach you love, love which wipes away all sins and makes you perfect, love which gives you the peace of my Son now and forever. Peace with you and in you, because I am the Queen of Peace. Thank you."

SEPTEMBER 2, 2010

"Dear children, I am beside you because I desire to help you to overcome trials, which this time of purification puts before you. My children, one of those is not to forgive and not to ask for forgiveness. Every sin offends Love and distances you from it – and Love is my Son. Therefore, my children, if you desire to walk with me towards the peace of God's love, you must learn to forgive and to ask for forgiveness. Thank you."

❧ CHAPTER 68 ☙
MARY'S IMMACULATE HEART

NOVEMBER 25, 1994

"Dear children! Today I call you to prayer. I am with you and I love you all. I am your Mother and I wish that your hearts be similar to my heart. Little children, without prayer you cannot live and say that you are mine. Prayer is joy. Prayer is what the human heart desires. Therefore, get closer, little children, to my Immaculate Heart and you will discover God. Thank you for having responded to my call."

MAY 25, 1995

"Dear Children! I invite you, little children, to help me through your prayers so that as many hearts as possible come close to my Immaculate Heart. Satan is strong and with all his forces wants to bring closer the most people possible to himself and to sin. That is why he is on the prowl to snatch more every moment. I beg you, little children, pray and help me to help you. I am your mother and I love you and that is why I wish to help you. Thank you for having responded to my call."

OCTOBER 25, 1996

"Dear children! Today I invite you to open yourselves to God the Creator, so that He changes you. Little children, you are dear to me. I love you all and I call you to be closer to me and that your love towards my Immaculate Heart be more fervent. I wish to renew you and lead you with my Heart to the Heart of Jesus, which still today suffers for you and calls you to conversion and renewal. Through you, I wish to renew the world. Comprehend, little children, that you are today the salt of the earth and the light of the world. Little children, I invite you and I love you and in a special way implore: Convert!" Thank you for having responded to my call."

SEPTEMBER 25, 2009

"Dear children, with joy, persistently work on your conversion. Offer all your joys and sorrows to my Immaculate Heart that I may lead you all to my most beloved Son, so that you may find joy in His Heart. I am with you to instruct you and to lead you towards eternity. Thank you for having responded to my call."

❧ CHAPTER 69 ❦
MARY'S JOY

AUGUST 14, 1986

"Dear children! My call to you is that your prayer be the joy of an encounter with the Lord. I am not able to guide you as long as you yourselves do not experience joy in prayer. From day to day I desire to lead you more and more in prayer, but I do not wish to force you. Thank you for having responded to my call."

DECEMBER 11, 1986

"Dear children! I am calling you to pray especially at this time in order to experience the joy of meeting with the new-born Jesus. Dear children, I desire that you experience these days just as I experience them. With joy I wish to guide you and show you the joy into which I desire to bring each one of you. Therefore, dear children, pray and surrender completely to me. Thank you for having responded to my call."

JUNE 25, 1995

"Dear Children! Today I am happy to see you in such great numbers, that you have responded and have come to live my messages. I invite you, little children, to be my joyful carriers of peace in this troubled world. Pray for peace so that as soon as possible a time of peace, which my heart waits impatiently for, may reign. I am near to you, little children, and intercede for every one of you before the Most High. I bless you with my motherly blessing. Thank you for having responded to my call."

DECEMBER 25, 1998

"Dear children! Today, on the birthday of my Son, my heart is filled with immeasurable joy, love and peace. As your mother, I desire for each of you to feel that same joy, peace and love in the heart. That is why do not be afraid to open your heart and to completely surrender yourself to Jesus, because only in this way can He enter into your heart and fill it with love, peace and joy. I bless you with my motherly blessing."

AUGUST 25, 2000

"Dear children! I desire to share my joy with you. In my Immaculate Heart I feel that there are many of those who have drawn closer to me and are, in a special way, carrying the victory of my Immaculate Heart in their hearts by praying and converting. I desire to thank you and to inspire you to work even more for God and His kingdom with love and the power of the Holy Spirit. I am with you and I bless you with my motherly blessing. Thank you for having responded to my call."

JUNE 25, 2006

"Dear children! With great joy in my heart I thank you for all the prayers that, in these days, you offered for my intentions. Know, little children, that you will not regret it, neither you nor your children. God will reward you with great graces and you will merit eternal life. I am near you and thank all those who, through these years, have accepted my messages, have poured them into their life and decided for holiness and peace. Thank you for having responded to my call."

JUNE 25, 2011

"Dear children! Give thanks with me to the Most High for my presence with you. My heart is joyful watching the love and joy in the living of my messages. Many of you have responded, but I wait for, and seek, all the hearts that have fallen asleep to awaken from the sleep of unbelief. Little children, draw even closer to my Immaculate Heart so that I can lead all of you toward eternity. Thank you for having responded to my call."

҈ CHAPTER 70 ҉
MARY'S PRAYER FOR US

FEBRUARY 25, 1994

"Dear children! Today I thank you for your prayers. All of you have helped me so that this war may end as soon as possible. I am close to you and I pray for each one of you and I beg you: pray, pray, pray. Only through prayer can we defeat evil and protect all that Satan wants to destroy in your lives. I am your Mother and I love you all equally, and I intercede for you before God. Thank you for having responded to my call."

OCTOBER 25, 2011

"Dear children! I am looking at you and in your hearts I do not see joy. Today I desire to give you the joy of the Risen One, that He may lead you and embrace you with His love and tenderness. I love you and I am praying for your conversion without ceasing before my Son Jesus. Thank you for having responded to my call."

❧ CHAPTER 71 ❦
MARY'S PROTECTION

JULY 11, 1985

"Dear children! I love the parish and with my mantle I protect it from every work of Satan. Pray that Satan retreats from the parish and from every individual who comes into the parish. In that way you shall be able to hear every call of God and answer it with your life. Thank you for having responded to my call."

AUGUST 1, 1985

"Dear children! I wish to tell you that I have chosen this parish and that I am guarding it in my hands like a little flower that does not want to die. I call you to surrender to me so that I can keep on presenting you to God, fresh and without sin. Satan has taken part of the plan and wants to possess it. Pray that he does not succeed in that, because I wish you for myself so I can keep on giving you to God. Thank you for having responded to my call."

AUGUST 25, 1990

"Dear children! I desire to invite you to take with seriousness and put into practice the messages which I am giving you. You know, little children, that I am with you and I desire to lead you along the same path to heaven, which is beautiful for those who discover it in prayer. Therefore, little children, do not forget that those messages which I am giving you have to be put into your everyday life in order that you might be able to say: "There, I have taken the messages and tried to live them." Dear children, I am protecting you before the heavenly Father by my own prayers. Thank you for having responded to my call."

SEPTEMBER 25, 1990

"Dear children! I invite you to pray with the heart in order that your prayer may be a conversation with God. I desire each one of you to dedicate more time to God. Satan is strong and wants to destroy and deceive you in many ways. Therefore, dear children, pray every day that your life will be good for yourselves and for all those you meet. I am with you and I am protecting you even though Satan wishes to destroy my plans and to hinder the desires which the Heavenly Father wants to realize here. Thank you for having responded to my call."

DECEMBER 25, 1992

"Dear children! I desire to place all of you under my mantle and protect you from all satanic attacks. Today is a day of peace, but in the whole world there is a great lack of peace. That is why I call you all to build a new world of peace with me through prayer. This I cannot do without you, and this is why I call all of you with my motherly love and God will do the rest. So, open yourselves to God's plan and to His designs to be able to cooperate with Him for peace and for everything that is good. Do not forget that your life does not belong to you, but is a gift with which you must bring joy to others and lead them to eternal life. May the tenderness of the little Jesus always accompany you. Thank you for having responded to my call."

JUNE 25, 1993

"Dear children! Today I also rejoice at your presence here. I bless you with my motherly blessing and intercede for each one of you before God. I call you anew to live my messages and to put them into life and practice. I am with you and bless all of you day by day. Dear children, these are special times and, therefore, I am with you to love and protect you; to protect your hearts from Satan and to bring you all closer to the heart of my Son, Jesus. Thank you for having responded to my call."

❧ CHAPTER 72 ❧
MARY'S THANKS

NOVEMBER 28, 1985

"Dear children! I want to thank everyone for all you have done for me, especially the youth. I beseech you, dear children, come to prayer with awareness. In prayer you shall come to know the greatness of God. Thank you for having responded to my call."

DECEMBER 26, 1985

"Dear children! I wish to thank all who have listened to my messages and who on Christmas Day have lived what I said. Undefiled by sin from now on, I wish to lead you further in love. Abandon your hearts to me! Thank you for having responded to my call!"

MARCH 13, 1986

"Dear children! Today I call you to live Lent by means of your little sacrifices. Thank you for every sacrifice you have brought me. Dear children, live that way continuously, and with your love help me to present the sacrifice. God will reward you for that. Thank you for having responded to my call."

AUGUST 21, 1986

"Dear children! I thank you for the love which you are showing me. You know, dear children, that I love you immeasurably and daily I pray the Lord to help you to understand the love which I am showing you. Therefore, you, dear children, pray, pray, pray!"

DECEMBER 25, 1986 (CHRISTMAS DAY)

"Dear children! Today also I give thanks to the Lord for all that He is doing for me, especially for this gift that I am able to be with you also today. Dear children, these are the days in which the Father grants special graces to all who open their hearts. I bless you and I desire that you too, dear children, become alive to the graces and place everything at God's disposal so that He may be glorified through you. My heart carefully follows your progress. Thank you for having responded to my call."

JANUARY 8, 1987

"Dear children! I desire to thank you for every response to the messages. Especially, dear children, thank you for all the sacrifices and prayers which you have presented to me. Dear children, I desire to keep on giving you still further messages, only not every Thursday, dear children, but on each 25th in the month. The time has come when what my Lord desired has been fulfilled. Now I will give you less messages, but I am still with you. Therefore, dear children, I beseech you, listen to my messages and live them, so I can guide you. Dear children, thank you for having responded to my call."

JUNE 25, 1987

"Dear children! Today I thank you and I want to invite you all to God's peace. I want each one of you to experience in your heart that peace which God gives. I want to bless you all today. I am blessing you with God's blessing and I beseech you, dear children, to follow and to live my way. I love you, dear children, and so not even counting the number of times, I go on calling you and I thank you for all that you are doing for my intentions. I beg you, help me to present you to God and to save you. Thank you for having responded to my call."

JUNE 25, 1990

"Dear children! Today I desire to thank you for all your sacrifices and for all your prayers. I am blessing you with my special motherly blessing. I invite you all to decide for God, so that from day to day you will discover His will in prayer. I desire, dear children, to call all of you to a full conversion so that joy will be in your hearts. I am happy that you are here today in such great numbers. Thank you for having responded to my call."

MAY 25, 1996

"Dear children! Today I wish to thank you for all your prayers and sacrifices that you, during this month which is consecrated to me, have offered to me. Little children, I also wish that you all become active during this time that is through me connected to heaven in a special way. Pray in order to understand that you all, through your life and your example, ought to collaborate in the work of salvation. Little children, I wish that all people convert and see me and my son, Jesus, in you. I will intercede for you and help you to become the light. In helping the other, your soul will also find salvation. Thank you for having responded to my call."

JUNE 25, 1996

"Dear children! Today I thank you for all the sacrifices you have offered me these days. Little children, I invite you to open yourselves to me and to decide for conversion. Your hearts, little children, are still not completely open to me and therefore, I invite you again to open to prayer so that in prayer the Holy Spirit will help you, that your hearts become of flesh and not of stone. Little children, thank you for having responded to my call and for having decided to walk with me toward holiness."

JUNE 25, 1998

"Dear children! Today I desire to thank you for living my messages. I bless you all with my motherly blessing and I bring you all before my Son Jesus. Thank you for having responded to my call."

JUNE 25, 2005

"Dear children! Today I thank you for every sacrifice that you have offered for my intentions. I call you, little children, to be my apostles of peace and love in your families and in the world. Pray that the Holy Spirit may enlighten and lead you on the way of holiness. I am with you and bless you all with my motherly blessing. Thank you for having responded to my call."

JUNE 25, 2006

"Dear children! With great joy in my heart I thank you for all the prayers that, in these days, you offered for my intentions. Know, little children, that you will not regret it, neither you nor your children. God will reward you with great graces and you will merit eternal life. I am near you and thank all those who, through these years, have accepted my messages, have poured them into their life and decided for holiness and peace. Thank you for having responded to my call."

❧ CHAPTER 73 ❧
MAY JESUS BE THE MEANING OF YOUR LIFE

MARCH 2, 2008

"Dear children, I implore you, especially at this Lenten time, to respond to God's goodness because He chose you and sent me among you. Be purified of sins and in Jesus, my Son, recognize the sacrifice of atonement

for the sins of the entire world. May He be the meaning of your life.
May your life become service to the Divine Love of my Son. Thank you
my children."

❧ CHAPTER 74 ❧
YEARLY MESSAGES TO IVANKA

Ivanka Ivankovic-Elez had daily apparitions from June 24, 1981 to May
7, 1985. On that day, Our Lady told her:

"My dear child, today is our last meeting, but do not be sad because I will
come to you on every anniversary except this one. My child, do not
think that you have done something wrong, and that's why I no longer
come. No, this isn't true. The plan which my Son and I have, you
accepted with all your heart and completed your part. Be happy because
I am your mother and I love you with all my heart. Ivanka, thank you
for having responded to the invitation of my Son and for persevering and
for always being close to Him and staying until He had completed that
for which He asked of You. My child, tell your friends that both I and
my Son will always be there for you when you seek or call us. That which I
told you during these years about the secrets, it is still not time to tell
anyone. Ivanka, the grace which you and the others received, nobody on
this earth has received up until now!"

Confiding to her the tenth secret, Our Lady told her that for the rest of
her life, she would have one yearly apparition on June 25, the anniversary
of the apparitions.

JUNE 25, 1995
"Our Lady blessed everyone present at the apparition. She spoke to me
about the secrets. She called us to pray for families because Satan desires
to destroy them. In addition, Our Lady called on all people to be
messengers of peace."

JUNE 25, 1996

The apparition took place in her family home, and lasted seven minutes. After the apparition, Ivanka said that this had been one of the most beautiful apparitions that she had had up to the present. As well as this, Our Lady thanks us for our prayer and for our love and desires that prayer and love become interwoven into every day. In conclusion, she invited us to pray for those who were under diabolic possession.

JUNE 25, 1997

"Our Lady talked to me about the fifth secret and spoke the following message: "Dear children, pray with the heart to know how to forgive and how to be forgiven. I thank you for your prayers and the love you give to me."

JUNE 25, 1998

"Our Lady was joyful. I asked her to bless everyone, which she did. Our Lady talked to me about all the secrets. She invited us to pray for the families at this time and especially to pray for the sick. She called us to open our hearts and to thank her son for the grace He has given us. At the end, Our Lady thanked us for our prayers and love."

JUNE 25, 1999

"Dear children, thank my Son for all the graces that he has given you. Pray for peace, pray for peace, pray for peace!"

JUNE 25, 2000

"I introduced myself as "Queen of Peace." Again, I call you to peace, fasting, prayer. Renew family prayer and receive my blessing."

Ivanka told us that Our Lady was happy and that she spoke to her about the sixth secret.

JUNE 25, 2001

"Dear angels! Thank you for your prayers, because through them my plan is being realized. This is why, angels, pray, pray, pray, so that my plan may be realized. Receive my motherly blessing!"

JUNE 25, 2002

"Dear Children, do not tire of prayer. Pray for peace, peace, peace."

Our Lady related to Ivanka some new details about her life. She gave us her motherly blessing. Our Lady was joyful.

JUNE 25, 2003

"Dear children! Do not be afraid, I am always with you. Open you heart for love and peace to enter into it. Pray for peace, peace, peace."

JUNE 25, 2004

"Dear children! Pray for those families who have not come to know the love of my Son. Receive my motherly blessing."

Our Lady came joyful and spoke to Ivanka more extensively about her life.

JUNE 25, 2005

"Dear children, love each other with the love of my Son. Peace, peace, peace."

Our Lady was joyful and spoke to Ivanka about the 6th secret.

JUNE 25, 2006

"Dear children, thank you for having responded to my call. Pray, pray, pray."

Our Lady was joyful and spoke about the seventh secret.

JUNE 25, 2007

"Our Lady remained with me for 17 minutes. She was joyful and spoke to me about her life. Our Lady said: 'Dear children, receive my motherly blessing.'"

JUNE 25, 2008

"Our Lady spoke to me about the ninth secret. She gave us her motherly blessing."

JUNE 25, 2009

"Our Lady remained with me for 10 minutes and spoke to me of the tenth secret. Our Lady said: 'Dear children, I call you to be apostles of peace. Peace, peace, peace.'"

JUNE 25, 2010

The apparition, which lasted 6 minutes, took place at Ivanka's family home. Only Ivanka's family was present at the apparition. After the apparition, Ivanka said: "Our Lady spoke to me about the fifth secret and, at the end, said: 'Dear children, receive my motherly blessing.'"

JUNE 25, 2011

The apparition, which lasted 8 minutes, took place at Ivanka's family home. Only Ivanka's family was present at the apparition. After the apparition, Ivanka said: "Our Lady spoke to me about the first secret and, at the end, said: "Dear children, receive my motherly blessing.'"

∂◦ CHAPTER 75 ◦ぅ
YEARLY MESSAGES TO JAKOV

Jakov Colo had daily apparitions from June 25, 1981 to September 12, 1998. On that day, Our Lady told him:

"Dear child! I am your mother and I love you unconditionally. From today, I will not be appearing to you every day, but only on Christmas, the birthday of my Son. Do not be sad, because as a mother, I will always be with you and like every true mother, I will never leave you. And you continue further to follow the way of my Son, the way of peace and love and try to persevere in the mission that I have confided to you. Be an example of that man who has known God and God's love. Let people always see in you and example of how God acts on people and how God acts through them. I bless you with my motherly blessing and I thank you for having responded to my call."

Entrusting to him the tenth secret, Our Lady told him that for the rest of his life he would have one yearly apparition, on Christmas Day.

DECEMBER 25, 1998

Our Lady came joyful. She greeted me, as always, with 'Praised be Jesus!' She spoke to me about the secrets and afterwards gave me this message:

"Dear children! Today, on the birthday of my Son, my heart is filled with immeasurable joy, love and peace. As your mother, I desire for each of you to feel that same joy, peace and love in the heart. That is why do not be afraid to open your heart and to completely surrender yourself to Jesus, because only in this way can He enter into your heart and fill it with love, peace and joy. I bless you with my motherly blessing."

DECEMBER 25, 1999

"Dear children! Today on the birthday of my Son, when my heart is filled with immeasurable joy and love, I invite you to open fully and surrender fully to God. Throw out all the darkness from your heart and let God's light and God's love enter your heart and dwell there forever. Be carriers of God's light and love to all people, so everyone, in you and through you, can feel and experience the authentic light and love that only God is able to give you. I am blessing you with my motherly blessing!"

DECEMBER 25, 2000

She blessed everyone and gave a message:

"Dear children! Today when Jesus is born and by His birth brings immeasurable joy, love and peace, I call you, in a special way to say your yes to Jesus. Open your hearts so that Jesus enters into them, comes to dwell in them and starts to work through you. Only in this way will you be able to comprehend the true beauty of God's love, joy and peace. Dear children, rejoice in the birth of Jesus and pray for all those hearts that have not opened to Jesus so that Jesus may enter into each of their hearts and may start working through them, so that every person would be an example of a true person through whom God works."

DECEMBER 25, 2001

"Dear Children, today when Jesus is born anew for you, in a special way, I want to call you to conversion. Pray, pray, pray for the conversion of your heart, so that Jesus may be born in you all and may dwell in you and come to reign over your entire being. Thank you for having responded to the call."

DECEMBER 25, 2002

"Dear children! Today, on the day of love and peace, with Jesus in my arms, I call you to prayer for peace. Little children, without God and prayer you cannot have peace. Therefore, little children, open your heart so that the King of Peace may be born in your heart. Only in this way, you can witness and carry God's peace to this peaceless world. I am with you and bless you with my motherly blessing."

DECEMBER 25, 2003

"Dear children! Today, when in a special way, Jesus desires to give you His peace, I call you to pray for peace in your hearts. Children, without peace in your hearts you cannot feel the love and joy of the birth of Jesus. Therefore, little children, today in a special way, open your hearts and begin to pray. Only through prayer and complete surrender, will your heart be filled with the love and peace of Jesus. I bless you with my motherly blessing."

DECEMBER 25, 2004

"Dear children! Today, on a day of grace, with little Jesus in my arms, in a special way I call you to open your hearts and to start to pray. Little children, ask Jesus to be born in each of your hearts and to begin to rule in your lives. Pray to Him for the grace to be able to recognize Him always and in every person. Little children, ask Jesus for love, because only with God's love can you love God and all people. I carry you all in my heart and give you my Motherly blessing."

DECEMBER 25, 2005

"Dear children! Also today, in my arms I bring you little Jesus, the King of Peace, to bless you with His peace. Little children, in a special way today I call you to be my carriers of peace in this peaceless world. God will bless you. Little children, do not forget that I am your mother. I bless you all with a special blessing, with little Jesus in my arms. Thank you for having responded to my call."

DECEMBER 25, 2006

"Dear children! Also today I bring you the newborn Jesus in my arms. He who is the King of Heaven and earth, He is your peace. Little children, no one can give you peace as He who is the King of Peace. Therefore, adore Him in your hearts, choose Him and you will have joy in Him. He will bless you with His blessing of peace. Thank you for having responded to my call."

DECEMBER 25, 2007

"Dear children! Today, in a special way I call you to become open to God and for each of your hearts today to become a place of Jesus' birth. Little children, through all this time that God permits me to be with you, I desire to lead you to the joy of your life. Little children, the only true joy of your life is God. Therefore, dear children, do not seek joy in things of this earth but open your hearts and accept God. Little children, everything passes, only God remains in your heart. Thank you for having responded to my call."

DECEMBER 25, 2008

"Dear Children! Today, in a special way, I call you to pray for peace. Without God, you cannot have peace or live in peace. Therefore, little children, today on this day of grace, open your hearts to the King of Peace for Him to be born in you and to grant you His peace; and you, be carriers of peace in this peaceless world. Thank you for having responded to my call."

DECEMBER 25, 2009

"Dear children! All of this time in which God in a special way permits me to be with you, I desire to lead you on the way that leads to Jesus and to your salvation. My little children, you can find salvation only in God and therefore, especially on this day of grace with little Jesus in my arms, I call you to permit Jesus to be born in your hearts. Only with Jesus in your heart can you set out on the way of salvation and eternal life. Thank you for having responded to my call."

DECEMBER 25, 2010

At the last daily apparition to Jakov Colo on September 12, 1998, Our Lady told him that henceforth he would have one apparition a year, every December 25th, on Christmas Day. This is also how it was this year. The apparition began at 2:25 pm and lasted 7 minutes.

Jakov said: Our Lady spoke to me about the secrets and at the end said: "Pray, pray, pray."

DECEMBER 25, 2011

The apparition began at 3:30 pm and lasted 11 minutes. Our Lady's Message to Jakov:

"Dear children! Today, in a special way, I desire to take you to and give you over to my Son. Little children, open your hearts and permit Jesus to be born in you, because only in this way, little children, you yourselves will be able to experience your new birth and set out with Jesus in your hearts towards the way of salvation. Thank you for having responded to my call."

❧ CHAPTER 76 ❦
YEARLY MESSAGES TO MIRJANA

Mirjana Dragicevic-Soldo had daily apparitions from June 24, 1981 to December 25, 1982. On that day, Our Lady told her:

"Mirjana, I chose you, and I told you everything that is necessary. I entrusted you with the knowledge of many abominations, which you must carry with dignity. Think of me, and how much I too shed tears because of this. You must always be brave. You quickly understood my messages, and so you must understand that now I must leave. Be brave...!"

Entrusting to her the tenth secret, Our Lady told her that for the rest of her life she would have one yearly apparition, on March 18th.

MARCH 18, 1995

"Dear children! Already for many years as a Mother, I have been teaching you faith and God's love. You have not shown gratitude to the dear Father nor have you given him glory. You have become empty and your heart has become hard and without love toward your neighbors' sufferings. I am teaching you love and showing you that the dear Father loved you but you have not loved him. He sacrificed his Son for your salvation, my children. As long as you do not love, you will not know your Father's love. You won't get to know him because God is love. Love and don't be afraid, my children, because there is no fear in love. If your hearts are open to the Father and if they are full of love toward him, then why any fear of what is to come? Those who are afraid are the ones who do not love because they are waiting for punishments and because they know how empty and hard they are. Children, I am leading you to love, to the dear Father. I am leading you to eternal life. Eternal life is my Son. Receive him and you have received love."

MARCH 18, 1996

"Dear children! On this message, which I give you today through my servant, I desire for you to reflect a long time. My children, great is the love of God. Do not close your eyes, do not close your ears, while I repeat to you: Great is His love! Hear my call and my supplication, which I direct to you. Consecrate your heart and make in it the home of the Lord. May he dwell in it forever. My eyes and my heart will be here, even when I will no longer appear. Act in everything as I ask you and lead you to the Lord. Do not reject from yourself the name of God, that you may not be rejected. Accept my messages that you may be accepted. Decide, my children, it is the time of decision. Be of just and innocent heart that I may lead you to your Father, for this that I am here, in His great love. Thank you for being here!"

MARCH 18, 1997

"Dear children! As a mother I beseech you, do not go on the way you have been going. That is a way without love toward neighbor and toward my Son. On that way, you will find only hardness and emptiness of heart, and not the peace that everyone is crying out for. Genuine peace will be had only by the one who sees and loves my Son in his neighbor. In whose heart my Son reigns, that one knows what peace is and tranquility. Thank you having responded to my call."

MARCH 18, 1998

"Dear children! I call you to be my light, in order to enlighten all those who still live in darkness, to fill their hearts with Peace, my Son. Thank you for having responded to my call!"

MARCH 18, 1999

"Dear children! I want you to surrender your hearts to me so that I may take you on the way, which leads to the light and to eternal life. I do not want your hearts to wander in today's darkness. I will help you. I will be with you on this way of discovery of the love and the mercy of God. As a mother, I ask you to permit me to do this. Thank you for having responded to my call."

MARCH 18, 2000

"Dear children! Do not seek peace and happiness in vain, in the wrong places and in wrong things. Do not permit your hearts to become hard by loving vanity. Invoke the name of my Son. Receive Him in your heart. Only in the name of my Son will you experience true happiness and true peace in your heart. Only in this way will you come to know the love of God and spread it further. I am calling you to be my apostles."

MARCH 18, 2001

"Dear children! Today I call you to love and mercy. Give love to each other as your Father gives it to you. Be merciful (pause) - with the heart. Do good works, not permitting them to wait for you too long. Every mercy that comes from the heart brings you closer to my Son."

MARCH 18, 2002

"Dear children! As a mother, I implore you, open your heart and offer it to me, and fear nothing. I will be with you and will teach you how to put Jesus in the first place. I will teach you to love Him and to belong to Him completely. Comprehend, dear children, that without my Son there is no salvation. You should become aware that He is your beginning and your end. Only with this awareness can you be happy and merit eternal life. As your mother, I desire this for you. Thank you for having responded to my call."

MARCH 18, 2003

"Dear children! Particularly at this holy time of penance and prayer, I call you to make a choice. God gave you free will to choose life or death. Listen to my messages with the heart that you may become cognizant of what you are to do and how you will find the way to life. My children, without God you can do nothing; do not forget this even for a single moment. For, what are you and what will you be on earth, when you will return to it again. Do not anger God, but follow me to life. Thank you for being here."

MARCH 18, 2004

"Dear children! Also today, watching you with a heart full of love, I desire to tell you that what you persistently seek, what you long for, my little children, is before you. It is sufficient that, in a cleaned heart, you place my Son in the first place, and then you will be able to see. Listen to me and permit me to lead you to this in a motherly way."

MARCH 18, 2005

"Dear children! I come to you as the mother who, above all, loves her children. My children, I desire to teach you to love also. I pray for this. I pray that you will recognize my Son in each of your neighbors. The way to my Son, who is true peace and love, passes through the love for all neighbors. My children, pray and fast for your heart to be open for this my intention."

MARCH 18, 2006

"Dear children! In this Lenten time, I call you to interior renunciation. The way to this leads you through love, fasting, prayer and good works. Only with total interior renunciation will you recognize God's love and the signs of the time in which you live. You will be witnesses of these signs and will begin to speak about them. I desire to bring you to this. Thank you for having responded to me."

MARCH 18, 2007

"Dear children! I come to you as a Mother with gifts. I come with love and mercy. Dear children, mine is a big heart. In it, I desire all of your hearts, purified by fasting and prayer. I desire that, through love, our hearts may triumph together. I desire that through that triumph you may see the real Truth, the real Way and the real Life. I desire that you may see my Son. Thank you."

MARCH 18, 2008

I have never seen Our Lady address us in this manner. She extended her hands towards us and with her hands extended in this way, she said:

"Dear children, today I extend my hands towards you. Do not be afraid to accept them. They desire to give you love and peace and to help you in salvation. Therefore, my children, receive them. Fill my heart with joy and I will lead you towards holiness. The way on which I lead you is difficult and full of temptations and falls. I will be with you and my hands will hold you. Be persevering so that, at the end of the way, we can all together, in joy and love, hold the hands of my Son. Come with me; fear not. Thank you."

MARCH 18, 2009

"Dear children! Today I call you to look into your hearts sincerely and for a long time. What will you see in them? Where is my Son in them and where is the desire to follow me to Him? My children, may this time of renunciation be a time when you will ask yourself: 'What does my God desire of me personally? What am I to do?' Pray, fast and have a heart full of mercy. Do not forget your shepherds. Pray that they may not get lost, that they may remain in my Son so as to be good shepherds to their flock."

MARCH 18, 2010

"Dear children! Today I call you to love with all your heart and with all your soul. Pray for the gift of love, because when the soul loves it calls my Son to itself. My Son does not refuse those who call Him and who desire to live according to Him. Pray for those who do not comprehend love, who do not understand what it means to love. Pray that God may be their Father and not their Judge. My children, you be my apostles, be my river of love. I need you. Thank you."

MARCH 18, 2011

"Dear children! I am with you in the name of the greatest Love, in the name of dear God, who has come close to you through my Son and has shown you real love. I desire to lead you on the way of God. I desire to teach you real love so that others may see it in you, that you may see it in others, that you may be a brother to them and that others may see a merciful brother in you. My children, do not be afraid to open your hearts to me. With motherly love, I will show you what I expect of each of you, what I expect of my apostles. Set out with me. Thank you."

MARCH 18, 2012

"Dear children! I am coming among you because I desire to be your mother - your intercessor. I desire to be the bond between you and the Heavenly Father - your mediatrix. I desire to take you by the hand and to walk with you in the battle against the impure spirit. My children, consecrate yourselves to me completely. I will take your lives into my motherly hands and I will teach them peace and love, and then I will give them over to my Son. I am asking of you to pray and fast because only in this way will you know how to witness my Son in the right way through my motherly heart. Pray for your shepherds that, united in my Son, they can always joyfully proclaim the Word of God. Thank you."

❧ CHAPTER 77 ❧
HOLY MASS

MAY 16, 1985

"Dear children! I am calling you to a more active prayer and attendance at Holy Mass. I wish your Mass to be an experience of God. I wish especially to say to the young people: be open to the Holy Spirit because God wishes to draw you to Himself in these days when Satan is at work. Thank you for having responded to my call."

NOVEMBER 21, 1985

"Dear children! I want to tell you that this season is especially for you from the parish. When it is summer, you saw that you have a lot of work. Now you don't have work in the fields, work on your own self personally! Come to Mass because this is the season given to you. Dear children, there are enough of those who come regularly despite bad weather because they love me and wish to show their love in a special way. What I want from you is to show me your love by coming to Mass, and the Lord will reward you abundantly. Thank you for having responded to my call."

APRIL 3, 1986

"Dear children! I wish to call you to a living of the Holy Mass. There are many of you who have sensed the beauty of the Holy Mass, but there are also those who come unwillingly. I have chosen you, dear children, but Jesus gives you His graces in the Mass. Therefore, consciously live the Holy Mass and let your coming to it be a joyful one. Come to it with love and make the Mass your own. Thank you for having responded to my call."

JANUARY 25, 1998

"Dear children! Today again I call all of you to prayer. Only with prayer, dear children, will your heart change, become better, and be more sensitive to the Word of God. Little children, do not permit Satan to pull you apart and to do with you what he wants. I call you to be responsible and determined and to consecrate each day to God in prayer. May Holy Mass, little children, not be a habit for you, but life. By living Holy Mass each day, you will feel the need for holiness and you will grow in holiness. I am close to you and intercede before God for each of you, so that He may give you strength to change your heart. Thank you for having responded to my call."

AUGUST 2, 2008

"Dear children, In my coming to you, here among you, the greatness of God is reflected and the way with God to eternal joy is opening. Do not feel weak, alone or abandoned. Along with faith, prayer and love climb to the hill of salvation. May the Mass, the most exalted and most powerful act of your prayer, be the center of your spiritual life. Believe and love, my children. Those whom my Son chose and called will help you in this as well. To you and to them especially, I give my motherly blessing. Thank you."

❧ CHAPTER 78 ❧
MERCY OF GOD

APRIL 2, 2007

"Dear children, do not be of a hard heart towards the mercy of God, which has been pouring out upon you for so much of your time. In this special time of prayer, permit me to transform your hearts that you may help me to have my Son resurrect in all hearts, and that my heart may triumph. Thank you."

❧ CHAPTER 79 ❧
MIRACLES

MAY 25, 1993

"Dear children! Today I invite you to open yourselves to God by means of prayer so the Holy Spirit may begin to work miracles in you and through you. I am with you and I intercede before God for each one of you because, dear children, each one of you is important in my plan of salvation. I invite you to be carriers of good and peace. God can give you peace only if you convert and pray. Therefore, my dear little children, pray, pray, pray and do that which the Holy Spirit inspires you. Thank you for having responded to my call."

SEPTEMBER 25, 1993

"Dear children! I am your Mother and I invite you to come closer to God through prayer because only He is your peace, your savior. Therefore, little children, do not seek comfort in material things, but rather seek God. I am praying for you and I intercede before God for each individual. I am looking for your prayers that you accept me and accept my messages as in the first days of the apparitions and only then when you open your hearts and pray will miracles happen. Thank you for having responded to my call."

APRIL 25, 2001

"Dear children! Also today, I call you to prayer. Little children, prayer works miracles. When you are tired and sick and you do not know the meaning of your life, take the Rosary and pray; pray until prayer becomes for you a joyful meeting with your Savior. I am with you, little children, and I intercede and pray for you. Thank you for having responded to my call."

OCTOBER 25, 2002

"Dear children! Also today I call you to prayer. Little children, believe that by simple prayer miracles can be worked. Through your prayer you open your heart to God and He works miracles in your life. By looking at the fruits, your heart fills with joy and gratitude to God for everything He does in your life and, through you, also to others. Pray and believe little children, God gives you graces and you do not see them. Pray and you will see them. May your day be filled with prayer and thanksgiving for everything that God gives you. Thank you for having responded to my call."

❧ CHAPTER 80 ❧
MISSIONARIES OF THE MESSAGES

MAY 8, 1986

"Dear children! You are the ones responsible for the messages. The source of grace is here, but you, dear children, are the vessels which transport the gifts. Therefore, dear children, I am calling you to do your job with responsibility. Each one shall be responsible according to his own ability. Dear children, I am calling you to give the gifts to others with love, and not to keep them for yourselves. Thank you for having responded to my call."

FEBRUARY 25, 1995

"Dear children! Today I invite you to become missionaries of my messages, which I am giving here through this place that is dear to me. God has allowed me to stay this long with you and therefore, little children, I invite you to live with love the messages I give and to transmit them to the whole world, so that a river of love flows to people who are full of hatred and without peace. I invite you, little children, to become peace where there is no peace and light where there is darkness, so that each heart accepts the light and the way of salvation. Thank you for having responded to my call."

&ᴥ CHAPTER 81 ᴥ&
MOTHERLY BLESSING

AUGUST 15, 1985

"Dear children! Today I am blessing you and I wish to tell you that I love you and that I urge you to live my messages. Today I am blessing you with the solemn blessing that the Almighty grants me. Thank you for having responded to my call."

DECEMBER 19, 1985

"Dear children! Today I wish to call you to love of neighbor. The more you will to love your neighbor, the more you shall experience Jesus especially on Christmas Day. God will bestow great gifts on you if you surrender yourselves to Him. I wish in a special way on Christmas Day to give mothers my own special motherly blessing, and Jesus will bless the rest with His own blessing. Thank you for having responded to my call."

FEBRUARY 25, 1993

"Dear children! Today I bless you with my motherly blessing and I invite you all to conversion. I wish that each of you decide for a change of life and that each of you works more in the Church not through words and thoughts but through example, so that your life may be a joyful testimony for Jesus. You cannot say that you are converted, because your life must become a daily conversion. In order to understand what you have to do, little children, pray and God will give you what you completely have to do, and where you have to change. I am with you and place you all under my mantle. Thank you for having responded to my call."

DECEMBER 25, 1998

"Dear children! In this Christmas joy I desire to bless you with my blessing. In a special way, little children, I give you the blessing of little Jesus. May He fill you with His peace. Today, little children, you do not have peace and yet you yearn for it. That is why, with my Son Jesus, on this day I call you to pray, pray, pray, because without prayer you do not have joy or peace or a future. Yearn for peace and seek it, for God is true peace. Thank you for having responded to my call."

JUNE 25, 2001

"Dear children! I am with you and I bless you all with my motherly blessing. Especially today when God gives you abundant graces, pray and seek God through me. God gives you great graces, that is why, little children make good use of this time of grace and come closer to my heart so that I can lead you to my Son Jesus. Thank you for having responded to my call."

DECEMBER 25, 2003

"Dear children! Also today, I bless you all with my Son Jesus in my arms and I carry Him, who is the King of Peace, to you, that He grant you His peace. I am with you and I love you all, little children. Thank you for having responded to my call."

MARCH 25, 2011

"Dear children! In a special way today I desire to call you to conversion. As of today, may new life begin in your heart. Children, I desire to see your 'yes', and may your life be a joyful living of God's will at every moment of your life. In a special way today, I bless you with my motherly blessing of peace, love and unity in my heart and in the heart of my Son Jesus. Thank you for having responded to my call."

❧ CHAPTER 82 ❦
MY CHILDREN, BE HUMBLE.

DECEMBER 2, 2008

"Dear children! In this holy time of joyful expectation, God has chosen you, the little ones, to realize His great intentions. My children, be humble. Through your humility, with His wisdom, God will make of your souls a chosen home. You will illuminate it with good works and thus, with an open heart, you will welcome the birth of my Son in all of His generous love. Thank you, dear children."

❧ CHAPTER 83 ❦
MY CHILDREN, HELP ME; I WILL TRIUMPH.

MAY 2, 2006

"Dear Children, I am coming to you as a mother. I am coming with an open heart full of love for you, my children. Cleanse your hearts from everything that prevents you from receiving me; from recognizing the love of my Son. Through you, my heart desires to win – desires to triumph. Open your hearts; I will lead you to this. Thank you!"

OCTOBER 2, 2010

"Dear children! Today I call you to a humble, my children, humble devotion. Your hearts need to be just. May your crosses be your means in the battle against the sins of the present time. May your weapon be patience and boundless love – a love that knows to wait and which will make you capable of recognizing God's signs – that your life, by humble love, may show the truth to all those who seek it in the darkness of lies. My children, my apostles, help me to open the paths to my Son. Once again I call you to pray for your shepherds. Alongside them, I will triumph. Thank you."

☙ CHAPTER 84 ❧
MY NAME IS LOVE

MARCH 2, 2007

"Today I will speak to you about what you have forgotten. Dear children! My name is love. That I am with you for so much of your time is love, because the Great Love sends me. I am asking the same of you. I am asking for love in your families. I am asking that you recognize love in your brother. May fasting and prayer be your guiding star. Open your heart to love, namely, to salvation. Thank you."

☙ CHAPTER 85 ❧
MY SON – YOUR SAVIOR, YOUR REDEEMER

APRIL 2, 2010

"Dear children! Today I bless you in a special way and I pray for you to return to the right way, to my Son - your Savior, your Redeemer – to Him who gave you eternal life. Reflect on everything human, on everything that does not permit you to set out after my Son – on transience, imperfection and limitation - and then think of my Son, of His Divine infiniteness. By your surrender and prayer ennoble your body and perfect your soul. Be ready, my children. Thank you."

Our Lady blessed all people and all the religious articles that we had for blessing. As Our Lady was leaving Mirjana saw a large golden Cross behind Our Lady.

&ъ CHAPTER 86 ๙

NO ONE IS LISTENING

JULY 25, 1985
"Dear children! I desire to lead you, but you do not wish to listen to my messages. Today I am calling you to listen to the messages and then you will be able to live everything which God tells me to convey to you. Open yourselves to God and God will work through you and keep on giving you everything you need. Thank you for having responded to my call."

&ъ CHAPTER 87 ๙

NON-BELIEVERS

NOVEMBER 25, 2003
"Dear children! I call you that this time be for you an even greater incentive to prayer. In this time, little children, pray that Jesus be born in all hearts, especially in those who do not know Him. Be love, joy and peace in this peaceless world. I am with you and intercede before God for each of you. Thank you for having responded to my call."

JANUARY 25, 2004
"Dear children! Also today I call you to pray. Pray, little children, in a special way for all those who have not come to know God's love. Pray that their hearts may open and draw closer to my heart and the Heart of my Son Jesus, so that we can transform them into people of peace and love. Thank you for having responded to my call."

NOVEMBER 25, 2004
"Dear children! At this time, I call you all to pray for my intentions. Especially, little children, pray for those who have not yet come to know the love of God and do not seek God the Savior. You, little children, be my extended hands and by your example draw them closer to my Heart and the Heart of my Son. God will reward you with graces and every blessing. Thank you for having responded to my call."

APRIL 2, 2006

"Dear Children, I am coming to you, because, with my own example, I wish to show you the importance of prayer for those who have not come to know the love of God. You ask yourself if you are following me? My children, do you not recognize the signs of the times? Do you not speak of them? Come follow me. As a mother I call you. Thank you for having responded."

FEBRUARY 25, 2008

"Dear children! In this time of grace, I call you anew to prayer and renunciation. May your day be interwoven with little ardent prayers for all those who have not come to know God's love. Thank you for having responded to my call."

FEBRUARY 2, 2010

"Dear children! With motherly love, today I call you to be a lighthouse to all souls who wander in the darkness of ignorance of God's love. That you may shine all the brighter and draw all the more souls, do not permit the untruths which come out of your mouth to silence your conscience. Be perfect. I am leading you with my motherly hand – a hand of love. Thank you."

NOVEMBER 2, 2011

"Dear children, the Father has not left you to yourselves. Immeasurable is His love, the love that is bringing me to you, to help you to come to know Him, so that, through my Son, all of you can call Him 'Father' with the fullness of heart; that you can be one people in God's family. However, my children, do not forget that you are not in this world only for yourselves, and that I am not calling you here only for your sake. Those who follow my Son think of the brother in Christ as of their very selves and they do not know selfishness. That is why I desire that you be the light of my Son, that to all those who have not come to know the Father - to all those who wander in the darkness of sin, despair, pain and loneliness - you may illuminate the way and that, with your life, you may show them the love of God. I am with you. If you open your hearts, I will lead you. Again I am calling you: pray for your shepherds. Thank you."

&❧ CHAPTER 88 ❦&
ONLY THROUGH THE LOVE OF GOD

OCTOBER 2, 2006

"Dear children, I am coming to you in this your time, to direct the call to eternity to you. This is the call of love. I call you to love; because only through love will you come to know the love of God. Many think that they have faith in God and that they know his laws. They try to live according to them, but they do not do what is the most important; they do not love Him. My children, pray and fast. This is the way which will help you to open yourselves and to love. Only through the love of God is eternity gained. I am with you. I will lead you with the motherly love. Thank you for having responded." Our Lady added: "My children, priests' hands are blessed hands of my Son, respect them."

&❧ CHAPTER 89 ❦&
OUR LADY IS SADDENED

MAY 24, 1984

"Dear children! I have told you already that I have chosen you in a special way, just the way you are. I, the Mother, love you all. And in any moment that is difficult for you, do not be afraid! Because I love you even then when you are far from me and my Son. Please, do not let my heart weep with tears of blood because of the souls who are lost in sin. Therefore, dear children, pray, pray, pray! Thank you for having responded to my call."

OCTOBER 4, 1984

"Dear children! Today I want to tell you that again and again you make me happy by your prayer, but there are enough of those in this very parish who do not pray and my heart is saddened. Therefore pray that I can bring all your sacrifices and prayers to the Lord. Thank you for having responded to my call."

MARCH 2, 2011

"Dear children; My motherly heart suffers tremendously as I look at my children who persistently put what is human before what is of God; at my children who, despite everything that surrounds them and despite all the signs that are sent to them, think that they can walk without my Son. They cannot! They are walking to eternal perdition. That is why I am gathering you, who are ready to open your heart to me, you who are ready to be apostles of my love, to help me; so that by living God's love you may be an example to those who do not know it. May fasting and prayer give you strength in that and I bless you with motherly blessing in the name of the Father and of the Son and of the Holy Spirit. Thank you." Our Lady was very sad.

ॐ CHAPTER 90 ॐ
PEACE

SEPTEMBER 25, 1986

"Dear children! By your own peace I am calling you to help others to see and begin to seek peace. You, dear children, are at peace and not able to comprehend lack of peace. Therefore, I am calling you, so that by your prayer and your life you help to destroy everything that is evil in people and uncover the deception that Satan makes use of. You pray that the truth prevails in all hearts. Thank you for having responded to my call."

OCTOBER 23, 1986

"Dear children! Today again I am calling you to pray. Especially, dear children, do I call you to pray for peace. Without your prayers, dear children, I cannot help you to fulfill the message which the Lord has given me to give to you. Therefore, dear children, pray, so that in prayer you realize what God is giving you. Thank you for having responded to my call."

DECEMBER 25, 1988

"Dear children! I call you to peace. Live it in your heart and all around you, so that all will know peace, peace that does not come from you but from God. Little children, today is a great day. Rejoice with me. Glorify the Nativity of Jesus through the peace that I give you. It is for this peace that I have come as your Mother, Queen of Peace. Today I give you my special blessing. Bring it to all creation, so that all creation will know peace. Thank you for having responded to my call."

JULY 25, 1990

"Dear children! Today I invite you to peace. I have come here as the Queen of Peace and I desire to enrich you with my motherly peace. Dear children, I love you and I desire to bring all of you to the peace which only God gives and which enriches every heart. I invite you to become carriers and witnesses of my peace to this unpeaceful world. Let peace reign in the whole world which is without peace and longs for peace. I bless you with my motherly blessing. Thank you for having responded to my call."

OCTOBER 25, 1989

"Dear children! Today also I am inviting you to prayer. I am always inviting you, but you are still far away. Therefore, from today, decide seriously to dedicate time to God. I am with you and I wish to teach you to pray with the heart. In prayer with the heart you shall encounter God. Therefore, little children, pray, pray, pray! Thank you for having responded to my call."

OCTOBER 25, 1990

"Dear children! Today I call you to pray in a special way that you offer up sacrifices and good deeds for peace in the world. Satan is strong and with all his strength, desires to destroy the peace which comes from God. Therefore, dear children, pray in a special way with me for peace. I am with you and I desire to help you with my prayers and I desire to guide you on the path of peace. I bless you with my motherly blessing. Do not forget to live the messages of peace. Thank you for having responded to my call."

DECEMBER 25, 1990

"Dear children! Today I invite you in a special way to pray for peace. Dear children, without peace you cannot experience the birth of the little Jesus neither today nor in your daily lives. Therefore, pray the Lord of Peace that He may protect you with His mantle and that He may help you to comprehend the greatness and the importance of peace in your heart. In this way you shall be able to spread peace from your heart throughout the whole world. I am with you and I intercede for you before God. Pray, because Satan wants to destroy my plans of peace. Be reconciled with one another and by means of your lives help peace reign in the whole earth. Thank you for having responded to my call."

MARCH 25, 1993

"Dear children! Today like never I call you to pray for peace, for peace in your hearts, peace in your families and peace in the whole world, because Satan wants war, wants lack of peace, wants to destroy all which is good. Therefore, dear children, pray, pray, pray. Thank you for having responded to my call."

DECEMBER 25, 1994

"Dear children! Today I rejoice with you and I am praying with you for peace: peace in your hearts, peace in your families, peace in your desires, peace in the whole world. May the King of Peace bless you today and give you peace. I bless you and I carry each one of your in my heart. Thank you for having responded to my call."

MARCH 25, 1995

"Dear Children! Today I invite you to live the peace in your hearts and families. There is no peace, little children, where there is no prayer and there is no love, where there is no faith. Therefore, little children, I invite you all, to decide again today for conversion. I am close to you and I invite you all, little children, into my embrace to help you, but you do not want and in this way, Satan is tempting you, and in the smallest thing, your faith disappears. This is why little children, pray and through prayer, you will have blessing and peace. Thank you for having responded to my call."

DECEMBER 25, 1999

"Dear children! This is the time of grace. Little children, today in a special way with little Jesus, whom I hold in my embrace, I am giving you the possibility to decide for peace. Through your 'yes' for peace and your decision for God, a new possibility for peace is opened. Only in this way, little children, this century will be for you a time of peace and well-being. Therefore, put little newborn Jesus in the first place in your life and He will lead you on the way of salvation. Thank you for having responded to my call."

JANUARY 25, 2000

"Dear children! I call you, little children, to pray without ceasing. If you pray, you are closer to God and He will lead you on the way of peace and salvation. That is why I call you today to give peace to others. Only in God is there true peace. Open your hearts and become those who give a gift of peace and others will discover peace in you and through you and in this way you will witness God's peace and love which He gives you. Thank you for having responded to my call."

OCTOBER 25, 2001

"Dear children! Also today I call you to pray from your whole heart and to love each other. Little children, you are chosen to witness peace and joy. If there is no peace, pray and you will receive it. Through you and your prayer, little children, peace will begin to flow through the world. That is why, little children, pray, pray, pray, because prayer works miracles in human hearts and in the world. I am with you and I thank God for each of you who has accepted and lives prayer with seriousness. Thank you for having responded to my call."

DECEMBER 25, 2001

"Dear children! I call you today and encourage you to prayer for peace. Especially today I call you, carrying the newborn Jesus in my arms for you, to unite with Him through prayer and to become a sign to this peaceless world. Encourage each other, little children, to prayer and love. May your faith be an encouragement to others to believe and to love more. I bless you all and call you to be closer to my heart and to the heart of little Jesus. Thank you for having responded to my call."

SEPTEMBER 25, 2002

"Dear children! Also in this peaceless time, I call you to prayer. Little children, pray for peace so that in the world every person would feel love towards peace. Only when the soul finds peace in God, it feels content and love will begin to flow in the world. And in a special way, little children, you are called to live and witness peace; peace in your hearts and families, and through you, peace will also begin to flow in the world. Thank you for having responded to my call."

JANUARY 25, 2003

"Dear children! With this message I call you anew to pray for peace. Particularly now when peace is in crisis, you be those who pray and bear witness to peace. Little children, be peace in this peaceless world. Thank you for having responded to my call."

ANNUAL APPARITION TO JAKOV COLO · DECEMBER 25, 2003

"Dear children! Today, when in a special way, Jesus desires to give you His peace, I call you to pray for peace in your hearts. Children, without peace in your hearts you cannot feel the love and joy of the birth of Jesus. Therefore, little children, today in a special way, open your hearts and begin to pray. Only through prayer and complete surrender, will your heart be filled with the love and peace of Jesus. I bless you with my motherly blessing."

MAY 25, 2006

"Dear children! Also today I call you to put into practice and to live my messages that I am giving you. Decide for holiness, little children, and think of heaven. Only in this way, will you have peace in your heart that no one will be able to destroy. Peace is a gift, which God gives you in prayer. Little children, seek and work with all your strength for peace to win in your hearts and in the world. Thank you for having responded to my call."

NOVEMBER 25, 2008

"Dear children! Also today I call you, in this time of grace, to pray for little Jesus to be born in your heart. May He, who is peace itself, give peace to the entire world through you. Therefore, little children, pray without ceasing for this turbulent world without hope, so that you may become witnesses of peace for all. May hope begin to flow through your hearts as a river of grace. Thank you for having responded to my call."

APRIL 25, 2009

"Dear children! Today I call you all to pray for peace and to witness it in your families so that peace may become the highest treasure on this peaceless earth. I am your Queen of Peace and your mother. I desire to lead you on the way of peace, which comes only from God. Therefore, pray, pray, pray. Thank you for having responded to my call."

DECEMBER 25, 2010

"Dear children! Today, I and my Son desire to give you an abundance of joy and peace so that each of you may be a joyful carrier and witness of peace and joy in the places where you live. Little children, be a blessing and be peace. Thank you for having responded to my call."

DECEMBER 25, 2011

"Dear children! Also today, in my arms I am carrying my Son Jesus to you, for Him to give you His peace. Pray, little children, and witness so that in every heart, not human but God's peace may prevail, which no one can destroy. It is that peace in the heart which God gives to those whom He loves. By your baptism you are all, in a special way called and loved, therefore witness and pray that you may be my extended hands to this world which yearns for God and peace. Thank you for having responded to my call."

❧ CHAPTER 91 ❧
POPE JOHN PAUL II

AUGUST 25, 1994

"Dear children! Today I am united with you in prayer in a special way, praying for the gift of the presence of my most beloved son in your home country. Pray, little children, for the health of my most beloved son, who suffers, and whom I have chosen for these times. I pray and intercede before my Son, Jesus, so that the dream that your fathers had may be fulfilled. Pray, little children, in a special way, because Satan is strong and wants to destroy hope in your heart. I bless you. Thank you for having responded to my call."

&o CHAPTER 92 &
PRAY FOR MY INTENTIONS

JULY 25, 1993

"Dear children! I thank you for your prayers and for the love you show toward me. I invite you to decide to pray for my intentions. Dear children, offer novenas, making sacrifices wherein you feel the most bound. I want your life to be bound to me. I am your Mother, little children, and I do not want Satan to deceive you for He wants to lead you the wrong way, but he cannot if you do not permit him. Therefore, little children, renew prayer in your hearts, and then you will understand my call and my live desire to help you. Thank you for having responded to my call."

JULY 25, 2004

"Dear children! I call you anew: be open to my messages. I desire, little children, to draw you all closer to my Son Jesus; therefore, you pray and fast. Especially I call you to pray for my intentions, so that I can present you to my Son Jesus; for Him to transform and open your hearts to love. When you will have love in the heart, peace will rule in you. Thank you for having responded to my call."

NOVEMBER 25, 2004

"Dear children! At this time, I call you all to pray for my intentions. Especially, little children, pray for those who have not yet come to know the love of God and do not seek God the Savior. You, little children, be my extended hands and by your example draw them closer to my Heart and the Heart of my Son. God will reward you with graces and every blessing. Thank you for having responded to my call."

OCTOBER 25, 2008

"Dear children! In a special way I call you all to pray for my intentions so that, through your prayers, you may stop Satan's plan over this world, which is further from everyday, and which puts himself in the place of God and is destroying everything that is beautiful and good in the souls of each of you. Therefore, little children, arm yourselves with prayer and fasting so that you may be conscious of how much God loves you and may carry out God's will. Thank you for having responded to my call."

APRIL 25, 2010

"Dear children! At this time, when in a special way you are praying and seeking my intercession, I call you, little children, to pray so that through your prayers I can help you to have all the more hearts be opened to my messages. Pray for my intentions. I am with you and I intercede before my Son for each of you. Thank you for having responded to my call."

AUGUST 25, 2011

"Dear children! Today I call you to pray and fast for my intentions, because Satan wants to destroy my plan. Here I began with this parish and invited the entire world. Many have responded, but there is an enormous number of those who do not want to hear or accept my call. Therefore, you who have said 'yes', be strong and resolute. Thank you for having responded to my call."

❧ CHAPTER 93 ❧

PRAYER

APRIL 19, 1984 (HOLY THURSDAY)

"Dear children! Sympathize with me! Pray, pray, pray!"

MAY 24, 1984

"Dear children! I have told you already that I have chosen you in a special way, just the way you are. I, the Mother, love you all. And in any moment that is difficult for you, do not be afraid! Because I love you even then when you are far from me and my Son. Please, do not let my heart weep with tears of blood because of the souls who are lost in sin.

Therefore, dear children, pray, pray, pray!   Thank you for having responded to my call."

JUNE 21, 1984

"Pray, pray, pray! Thank you for having responded to my call."

SEPTEMBER 13, 1984

"Dear children! I still need your prayers. You wonder why all these prayers? Look around you, dear children, and you will see how greatly sin has dominated the world. Pray, therefore, that Jesus conquers. Thank you for having responded to my call."

NOVEMBER 15, 1984

"Dear children! You are a chosen people and God has given you great graces. You are not conscious of every message which I am giving you. Now I just want to say - pray, pray, pray! I don't know what else to tell you because I love you and I want you to comprehend my love and God's love through prayer. Thank you for having responded to my call."

MARCH 28, 1985

"Dear children! Today I wish to call you to pray, pray, pray! In prayer you shall perceive the greatest joy and the way out of every situation that has no exit. Thank you for starting up prayer. Each individual is dear to my heart. And I thank all who have urged prayer in their families. Thank you for having responded to my call."

MAY 30, 1985

"Dear children! I call you again to prayer with the heart. Let prayer, dear children, be your every day food in a special way when your work in the fields is so wearing you out that you cannot pray with the heart. Pray, and then you shall overcome even every weariness. Prayer will be your joy and your rest. Thank you for having responded to my call."

MARCH 20, 1986

"Dear children! Today I call you to approach prayer actively. You wish to live everything I am telling you, but you are not succeeding because you are not praying. Dear children, I beseech you to open yourselves and begin to pray. Prayer will be your joy. If you make a start, it won't be boring to you because you will be praying out of joy. Thank you for having responded to my call."

APRIL 24, 1986

"Dear children! Today my invitation is that you pray. Dear children, you are forgetting that you are all important. The elderly are especially important in the family. Urge them to pray. Let all the young people be an example to others by their life and let them witness to Jesus. Dear children, I beseech you, begin to change through prayer and you will know what you need to do. Thank you for having responded to my call."

JUNE 19, 1986

"Dear children! During these days my Lord is allowing me to be able to intercede more graces for you. Therefore, I wish to urge you once more to pray, dear children! Pray without ceasing! That way I will give you the joy which the Lord gives to me. With these graces, dear children, I want your sufferings to be a joy. I am your Mother and I desire to help you. Thank you for having responded to my call."

JULY 3, 1986

"Dear children! Today I am calling you all to prayer. Without prayer, dear children, you are not able to experience either God, or me or the graces which I am giving you. Therefore, my call to you is that the beginning and end of your day always be prayer. Dear children, I wish to lead you daily more and more in prayer, but you are not able to grow because you do not desire it. My call, dear children, is that for you prayer be in the first place. Thank you for having responded to my call."

AUGUST 14, 1986

"Dear children! My call to you is that your prayer be the joy of an encounter with the Lord. I am not able to guide you as long as you yourselves do not experience joy in prayer. From day to day I desire to lead you more and more in prayer, but I do not wish to force you. Thank you for having responded to my call."

OCTOBER 16, 1986

"Dear children! Today again I want to show you how much I love you, but I am sorry that I am not able to help each one to understand my love. Therefore, dear children, I am calling you to prayer and complete surrender to God, because Satan wants to sift you through everyday affairs and in your life he wants to snatch the first place. Therefore, dear children, pray without ceasing! Thank you for having responded to my call."

DECEMBER 18, 1986

"Dear children! Once again I desire to call you to prayer. When you pray you are much more beautiful, like flowers, which after the snow, show all their beauty and all their colors become indescribable. So also you, dear children, after prayer show before God all so much more what is beautiful and are beloved by Him. Therefore, dear children, pray and open your inner self to the Lord so that He makes of you a harmonious and beautiful flower for Paradise. Thank you for having responded to my call."

APRIL 25, 1987

"Dear children! Today also I am calling you to prayer. You know, dear children, that God grants special graces in prayer. Therefore, seek and pray in order that you may be able to comprehend all that I am giving here. I call you, dear children, to prayer with the heart. You know that without prayer you cannot comprehend all that God is planning through each one of you. Therefore, pray! I desire that through each one of you God's plan may be fulfilled, that all which God has planted in your heart may keep on growing. So pray that God's blessing may protect each one of you from all the evil that is threatening you. I bless you, dear children. Thank you for having responded to my call."

SEPTEMBER 25, 1987

"Dear children! Today also I want to call you all to prayer. Let prayer be your life. Dear children, dedicate your time only to Jesus and He will give you everything that you are seeking. He will reveal Himself to you in fullness. Dear children, Satan is strong and is waiting to test each one

Cross Mountain

The villagers erected a large cement Cross on top of Cross Mountain in 1933 to celebrate the 1900th anniversary of the Crucifixion. It is a great witness to Christ and can be seen from miles around. The climb up Cross Mountain is difficult and hazardous. The path is very rocky, jagged and steep. It is lined by the Stations of the Cross and at the top is a memorial to Fr. Slavko which marks the spot where he died. It takes about 45 minutes to an hour to prayerfully climb Cross Mountain and the sight from the top is well worth the effort. It is said that around sunrise of the day, some have seen Our Lady praying at the foot of the Cross.

Risen Christ

This beautiful bronze sculpture of Christ sits behind St. James Church on the walkway leading to Cross Mountain. As He rises from the tomb He leaves His imprint in the slab on the ground. The sculpture rises over twenty feet into the sky. This statue is a replica of the sculpture "The Resurrection" sculpted by Andrej Ajic.

A mysterious oil-like liquid has been dripping from the right knee of the Christ statue since 2001. Recently this liquid has also been flowing from the left leg. It has been claimed that this mysterious liquid has resulted in cures of sickness. Many pilgrims will stand in long lines to wait patiently for the opportunity to collect small drops of this liquid on hankerchiefs which can latter be given to those friends and family who are in need of healing. No determination has been made by the Vatican regarding the nature of this liquid.

Apparition Hill

This is the site where Our Lady of Medjugorje first appeared to two of the visionaries on June 24, 1981. The following day the six visionaries went to the hill with some of the villagers and the visionaries miraculously ascended the hill. The apparitions continued on the hill until the local government put a stop to that. Our Lady appeared for a period of time in St. James church, and in the parish rectory. She is currently appearing to the visionaries in their homes or wherever they may be.

Apparition hill is made up of jagged rocks and takes about thirty minutes to climb. The location where Our Lady first appeared was initially marked with a cross and many rocks stacked around the cross. Today, apparition hill is graced with a beautiful marble statue of Our Lady, which was donated by a Korean family, whose 10-year-old son was not able to speak from birth. His mother brought her boy to Medjugorje for a cure. After hearing his son speak for the first time as a result of a miracle, his father converted to Catholicism. The family later donated the beautiful marble statue in thanksgiving and dedicated the statue to Our Lady of Medjugorje.

St. James Church

The original church of St. James was built in 1897. A second church was built in 1969, and has been able to accommodate a larger number of pilgrims journeying to the village of Medjugorje.

In the early years of the apparitions, Our Lady appeared to the children in the choir loft or in the sacristy. Over forty million people from around the world have traveled to Medjugorje to worship and attend one of the many masses offered each day.

Millions of the Rosary and the Stations of the Cross have been prayed, millions of confessions have been heard, and millions of petitions have been presented to the open heart of the Blessed Virgin Mary. The church of St. James is truly an oasis of grace. There is a sense of peace and a feeling of being at home for the many pilgrims who have traveled there.

Vicka Ivankovic Mijatovic

She was born on September 3, 1964. Vicka is the oldest of the six visionaries. As of January 2013, she has received 9 of the 10 secrets and continues to see and speak with Our Lady daily. She and her husband Mario live with their two children a short distance from the village of Medjugorje. Our Lady has asked her to pray for the sick.

Marija Pavlovic Lunett

She was born on April 1, 1965. Marija saw Our Lady for the first time on June 25, 1981. As of January 2013, she is one of the three visionaries who continue to see and speak to Our Lady each day. Our Lady selected Marija to deliver her message on the 25th of each month to the world. The three visionaries who see Our Lady daily, have received nine of the ten secrets. Marija has married and has four children. Our Lady has asked her to pray for all the souls in purgatory.

Jakov Colo

He was born on March 6, 1971. He was 10 years old when the apparitions began. He is the youngest of the six visionaries. Both of his parents have died since the apparitions began. Our Lady adopted Jakov and assumed the role of his earthly mother as well as his spiritual mother. Thus it was very difficult for him when Our Lady told him that September 12, 1998 was the end of his daily apparitions. She promised to appear to him on December 25 every year. Jakov is married and lives with his wife and three children in the village of Medjugorje. Our Lady has asked Jakov to pray for the sick.

Ivan Dragicevic

He was born on May 25, 1965. He was there on June 24, 1981 and did see Our Lady briefly before running away frightened. As of January 2013, Our Lady continues to appear to him each day. He has received nine of the ten secrets that Our Lady has been giving to the visionaries. Our Lady revealed to Ivan that Pope John Paul II was with her in heaven, shortly after John Paul II died.

He married his wife Laureen and lives part of their time in Boston, MA, USA. They have three children. Our Lady has asked Ivan to pray for priests and the youth of the world.

Mirjana Dragicevic

She was born on March 18, 1965. Mirjana, along with Ivanka saw Our Lady on June 24, 1981. Our Lady did not speak to them and they were frightened and rushed home to tell the villagers what they had seen. Mirjana obtained a college degree from the University of Sarajevo. Our Lady continued to appear to her until December 25, 1982 when she received the tenth and final secret. Our Lady promised to appear to Mirjana on March 18 of each year (her birthday). Since August 2, 1987, Our Lady appears to Mirjana on the 2nd of each month. Initially the conversations were private, but currently Our Lady has made these messages public. Our Lady has asked Mirjana to pray for unbelievers.

Ivanka Ivankovic Eles

She was born on June 21, 1966. Ivanka and her companions, Mirjana and Ivan, were the first of the visionaries to see the Blessed Virgin Mary as they walked to their village in the afternoon on June 24, 1981, on the Feast of St. John the Baptist. Our Lady continued to appear to her until May 7, 1985 when she received the 10th and final secret. Our Lady promised to appear to her on June 25 of each year. Ivanka is currently married and has four children. Our Lady has asked her to pray for families.

Father Jozo Zouko

Father Jozo was the pastor of St. James Church when the apparitions began in June 1981. One day as the visionaries were running from the local police, Fr. Jozo heard the voice of Our Lady instructing him to "protect the children." He hid the children in the church and subsequently came to believe that the Mother of Jesus was appearing to the children. Within a few months he was arrested by the local police and imprisoned for two years. During which time he was tortured for refusing to deny the Medjugorje events.

He is currently one of the central religious figures of Medjugorje, traveling the world to share the messages and his convictions regarding the truth of Medjugorje.

Father Svetozar Kraljevic

Known as Father Svet to people around the world, he has been connected to Medjugorje and the apparitions from the early days.

Father Svet speaks fluent English and thus has been able to share the messages of Our Lady with the English speaking pilgrims.

He has also traveled extensively throughout the world to speak on these amazing events. He continues to live and work in the parish of St. James in Medjugorje.

Father Petar Ljubicic

Father Petar was in Medjugorje during the early days of the apparitions. He has been selected by Mirjana to reveal the contents of the secrets given to the visionaries. As Our Lady of Medjugorje permits, Mirjana will reveal the details of one secret at a time, ten days before the event takes place.

Father Petar will pray and fast on the secret for seven days. Three days before the secret event takes place, he will reveal the details to the world.

Father Petar has been located in a parish in Germany for many years, but recently in 2009, he has been transferred back to the parish of St. James in Medjugorje.

Father Slavko Barbaric

He was born on March 11, 1946. He was ordained to the priesthood on December 19, 1971. He was sent to Medjugorje in 1983 to investigate the events taking place. He became a spiritual advisor to the visionaries and a faithful believer and advocate of the continuing appearances of the Mother of God.

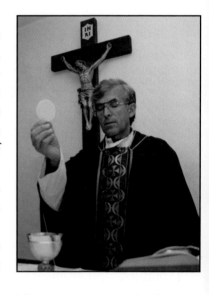

Father Slavko traveled the world to promote Medjugorje and to encourage all to embrace Our Lady's peace plan for the world. He wrote many spiritual books, which have been published in many languages to serve the many people throughout the world.

Every Friday he led prayer groups up Cross Mountain, reciting the Stations of the Cross. On a Friday as he was descending Cross Mountain, he blessed all the pilgrims with him and prayed with them the following prayer: "May Our Lady pray for us at the time of our death." He then very quickly died on that spot. A memorial has been placed at that location to remember this holy man. The following day after he died, Our Lady confirmed to the visionary Marija that Father Slavko was now with Her in heaven.

of you. Pray, and that way he will neither be able to injure you nor block you on the way of holiness. Dear children, through prayer grow all the more toward God from day to day. Thank you for having responded to my call."

NOVEMBER 25, 1988

"Dear children! I call you to prayer, to have an encounter with God in prayer. God gives Himself to you, but He wants you to answer in your own freedom to his invitation. That is why little children during the day, find yourself a special time when you could pray in peace and humility, and have this meeting with God the creator. I am with you and I intercede for you in front of God, so watch in vigil, so that every encounter in prayer be the joy of your contact with God. Thank you for having responded to my call."

FEBRUARY 25, 1989

"Dear children! Today I invite you to prayer of the heart. Throughout this season of grace I wish each of you to be united with Jesus, but without unceasing prayer you cannot experience the beauty and greatness of the grace which God is offering you. Therefore, little children, at all times fill your heart with even the smallest prayers. I am with you and unceasingly keep watch over every heart which is given to me. Thank you for having responded to my call."

AUGUST 25, 1989

"Dear children! I call you to prayer. By means of prayer, little children, you obtain joy and peace. Through prayer you are richer in the mercy of God. Therefore, little children, let prayer be the life of each one of you. Especially I call you to pray so that all those who are far away from God may be converted. Then our hearts shall be richer because God will rule in the hearts of all men. Therefore, little children, pray, pray, pray! Let prayers begin to rule in the whole world. Thank you for having responded to my call."

FEBRUARY 25, 1990

"Dear children! I invite you to surrender to God. In this season I specially want you to renounce all the things to which you are attached but which are hurting your spiritual life. Therefore, little children, decide completely for God, and do not allow Satan to come into your life through those things that hurt both you and your spiritual life. Little children, God is offering Himself to you in fullness, and you can discover and recognize Him only in prayer. Therefore make a decision for prayer. Thank you for having responded to call."

SEPTEMBER 25, 1990

"Dear children! I invite you to pray with the heart in order that your prayer may be a conversation with God. I desire each one of you to dedicate more time to God. Satan is strong and wants to destroy and deceive you in many ways. Therefore, dear children, pray every day that your life will be good for yourselves and for all those you meet. I am with you and I am protecting you even though Satan wishes to destroy my plans and to hinder the desires which the Heavenly Father wants to realize here. Thank you for having responded to my call."

JANUARY 25, 1991

"Dear children! Today, like never before, I invite you to prayer. Let your prayer be a prayer for peace. Satan is strong and desires to destroy not only human life, but also nature and the planet on which you live. Therefore, dear children, pray that through prayer you can protect yourselves with God's blessing of peace. God has sent me among you so that I may help you. If you so wish, grasp for the Rosary. Even the Rosary alone can work miracles in the world and in your lives. I bless you and I remain with you for as long as it is God's will. Thank you for not betraying my presence here and I thank you because your response is serving the good and the peace."

FEBRUARY 25, 1991

"Dear children! Today, I invite you to decide for God, because distance from God is the fruit of the lack of peace in your hearts. God is only peace. Therefore, approach Him through your personal prayer and then live peace in your hearts and in this way peace will flow from your hearts like a river into the whole world. Do not talk about peace, but make peace. I am blessing each of you and each good decision of yours. Thank you for having responded to my call."

MARCH 25, 1991

"Dear children! Again today I invite you to live the passion of Jesus in prayer, and in union with Him. Decide to give more time to God who gave you these days of grace. Therefore, dear children, pray and in a special way renew the love for Jesus for in your hearts. I am with you and I accompany you with my blessing and my prayers. Thank you for having responded to my call."

JULY 25, 1991

"Dear Children! Today I invite you to pray for peace. At this time peace is being threatened in a special way, and I am seeking from you to renew fasting and prayer in your families. Dear children, I desire you to grasp the seriousness of the situation and that much of what will happen depends on your prayers and you are praying a little bit. Dear children, I am with you and I am inviting you to begin to pray and fast seriously as in the first days of my coming. Thank you for having responded to my call."

AUGUST 25, 1991

"Dear Children! Today also I invite you to prayer, now as never before when my plan has begun to be realized. Satan is strong and wants to sweep away plans of peace and joy and make you think that my Son is not strong in his decisions. Therefore, I call all of you, dear children to pray and fast still more firmly. I invite you to realize through the secrets I began in Fatima may be fulfilled. I call you, dear children, to grasp the importance of my coming and the seriousness of the situation. I want to save all souls and present them to God. Therefore, let us pray that everything I have begun be fully realized. Thank you for having responded to my call."

OCTOBER 25, 1991

"Dear children! Pray! Pray! Pray!"

APRIL 25, 1992

"Dear children! Today also I invite you to prayer. Only by prayer and fasting can war be stopped. Therefore, my dear little children, pray and by your life give witness that you are mine and that you belong to me, because Satan wishes in these turbulent days to seduce as many souls as possible. Therefore, I invite you to decide for God and He will protect you and show you what you should do and which path to take. I invite all those who have said 'yes' to me to renew their consecration to my Son Jesus and to His Heart and to me so we can take you more intensely as instruments of peace in this unpeaceful world. Medjugorje is a sign to all of you and a call to pray and live the days of grace that God is giving you. Therefore, dear children, accept the call to prayer with seriousness. I am with you and your suffering is also mine. Thank you for having responded to my call."

MAY 25, 1992

"Dear children! Today also I invite you to prayer, so that through prayer you come still nearer to God. I am with you and I desire to lead you on the path to salvation that Jesus gives you. From day to day, I am nearer to you although you are not aware of it and you do not want to admit that you are only linked to me in a small way with your few prayers. When trials and problems arise, you say, "O God! O Mother! Where are you?" As for me, I only wait for your "Yes" to present to Jesus for Him to fill you with His grace. That is why, once more, please accept my call and start to pray in a new way until prayer becomes joy to you. Then you will discover that God is all-powerful in your daily life. I am with you and I am waiting for you. Thank you for having responded to my call."

JULY 25, 1992

"Dear children! Today also I invite you to prayer, a prayer of joy so that in these sad days no one amongst you may feel sadness in prayer, but a joyful meeting with God His Creator. Pray, little children, to be able to come closer to me and to feel through prayer what it is I desire from you. I am with you and each day I bless you with my maternal blessing so that Our Lord may fill you abundantly with His grace for your daily life. Give thanks to God for the grace of my being able to be with you because I assure you it is a great grace. Thank you for having responded to my call."

NOVEMBER 25, 1992

"Dear Children! Today, more than ever, I am calling you to pray. May your life become a continuous prayer. Without love you cannot pray. That is why I am calling you to love God, the Creator of your lives, above everything else. Then you will come to know God and will love Him in everything as He loves you. Dear children, it is a grace that I am with you. That is why you should accept and live my messages for your own good. I love you and that is why I am with you, in order to teach you and to lead you to a new life of conversion and renunciation. Only in this way will you discover God and all that which now seems so far away from you. Therefore, my dear children, pray. Thank you for having responded to my call."

DECEMBER 25, 1993

"Dear children! Today I rejoice with the little Jesus and I desire that Jesus' joy may enter into every heart. Little children, with the message I give you a blessing with my son Jesus, so that in every heart peace may reign. I love you, little children, and I invite all of your to come closer to me by means of prayer. You talk and talk but do not pray. Therefore, little children, decide for prayer. Only in this way will you be happy and God will give your what you seek from Him. Thank you for having responded to my call."

JANUARY 25, 1994

"Dear children! You are all my children. I love you. But, little children, you must not forget that without prayer you cannot be close to me. In these times Satan wants to create disorder in your hearts and in your families. Little children, do not give in. You should not allow him to lead you and your life. I love you and intercede before God for you. Little children, pray. Thank you for having responded to my call."

JULY 25, 1994

"Dear children! Today I invite you to decide to give time patiently for prayer. Little children, you cannot say you are mine and that you have experienced conversion through my messages if you are not ready to give time to God every day. I am close to you and I bless you all. Little children, do not forget that if you do not pray you are not close to me, nor are you close to the Holy Spirit who leads you along the path to holiness. Thank you for having responded to my call."

SEPTEMBER 25, 1994

"Dear children! I rejoice with you and I invite you to prayer. Little children, pray for my intention. Your prayers are necessary to me, through which I desire to bring you closer to God. He is your salvation. God sends me to help you and to guide you towards paradise, which is your goal. Therefore, little children, pray, pray, pray. Thank you for having responded to my call."

NOVEMBER 25, 1994

"Dear children! Today I call you to prayer. I am with you and I love you all. I am your Mother and I wish that your hearts be similar to my heart. Little children, without prayer you cannot live and say that you are mine. Prayer is joy. Prayer is what the human heart desires. Therefore, get closer, little children, to my Immaculate Heart and you will discover God. Thank you for having responded to my call."

JULY 25, 1995

"Dear children! Today I invite you to prayer because only in prayer can you understand my coming here. The Holy Spirit will enlighten you to understand that you must convert. Little children, I wish to make of you a most beautiful bouquet prepared for eternity but you do not accept the way of conversion, the way of salvation that I am offering you through these apparitions. Little children, pray, convert your hearts and come closer to me. May good overcome evil. I love you and bless you. Thank you for having responded to my call."

JUNE 25, 1997

"Dear children! Today I am with you in a special way and I bring you my motherly blessing of peace. I pray for you and I intercede for you before God, so that you may comprehend that each of you is a carrier of peace. You cannot have peace if your heart is not at peace with God. That is why, little children, pray, pray, pray, because prayer is the foundation of your peace. Open your heart and give time to God so that He will be your friend. When true friendship with God is realized, no storm can destroy it. Thank you for having responded to my call."

JULY 25, 1997

"Dear children! Today I invite you to respond to my call to prayer. I desire, dear children, that during this time you find a corner for personal prayer. I desire to lead you towards prayer with the heart. Only in this way will you comprehend that your life is empty without prayer. You will discover the meaning of your life when you discover God in prayer. That is why, little children, open the door of your heart and you will comprehend that prayer is joy without which you cannot live. Thank you for having responded to my call."

JANUARY 25, 1999

"Dear children! I again invite you to prayer. You have no excuse to work more because nature still lies in deep sleep. Open yourselves in prayer. Renew prayer in your families. Put Holy Scripture in a visible place in your families, read it, reflect on it and learn how God loves His people. His love shows itself also in present times because He sends me to call you upon the path of salvation. Thank you for having responded to my call."

JUNE 25, 2000

"Dear children! Today I call you to prayer. The one who prays is not afraid of the future. Little children do not forget, I am with you and I love you all. Thank you for having responded to my call."

APRIL 25, 2003

"Dear children! I call you also today to open yourselves to prayer. In the foregone time of Lent you have realized how small you are and how small your faith is. Little children, decide also today for God, that in you and through you He may change the hearts of people, and also your hearts. Be joyful carriers of the risen Jesus in this peaceless world, which yearns for God and for everything that is from God. I am with you, little children, and I love you with a special love. Thank you for having responded to my call."

JULY 25, 2009

"Dear children! May this time be a time of prayer for you. Thank you for having responded to my call. "

"Dear children! With great joy, also today, I desire to call you anew: pray, pray, pray. May this time be a time of personal prayer for you. During the day, find a place where you will pray joyfully in a recollected way. I love you and bless you all. Thank you for having responded to my call."

❧ CHAPTER 94 ❦
PRAYER BECOMES A JOY

NOVEMBER 25, 1999
"Dear children! Also today I call you to prayer. In this time of grace, may the cross be a sign-post of love and unity for you through which true peace comes. That is why, little children, pray especially at this time that little Jesus, the Creator of peace, may be born in your hearts. Only through prayer will you become my apostles of peace in this world without peace. That is why, pray until prayer becomes a joy for you. Thank you for having responded to my call."

JULY 25, 2003
"Dear children! Also today I call you to prayer. Little children, pray until prayer becomes a joy for you. Only in this way each of you will discover peace in the heart and your soul will be content. You will feel the need to witness to others the love that you feel in your heart and life. I am with you and intercede before God for all of you. Thank you for having responded to my call."

❧ CHAPTER 95 ❦
PRAYER GROUPS

SEPTEMBER 25, 2000
"Dear children! Today I call you to open yourselves to prayer. May prayer become joy for you. Renew prayer in your families and form

prayer groups.   In this way, you will experience joy in prayer and togetherness.   All those who pray and are members of prayer groups are open to God's will in their hearts and joyfully witness God's love.   I am with you, I carry all of you in my heart and I bless you with my motherly blessing.   Thank you for having responded to my call."

JUNE 25, 2004

"Dear children! Also today, joy is in my heart.   I desire to thank you for making my plan realizable.   Each of you is important, therefore, little children, pray and rejoice with me for every heart that has converted and become an instrument of peace in the world.   Prayer groups are powerful, and through them I can see, little children, that the Holy Spirit is at work in the world.   Thank you for having responded to my call."

☙ CHAPTER 96 ❧
PRAYER WITH THE HEART

JANUARY 23, 1986

"Dear children! Again I call you to prayer with the heart.   If you pray with the heart, dear children, the ice of your brothers will melt and every barrier shall disappear.   Conversion will be easy for all who desire to accept it.   That is the gift which by prayer you must obtain for your neighbor.   Thank you for having responded to my call."

AUGUST 28, 1986

"Dear children! My call is that in everything you would be an image for others, especially in prayer and witnessing.   Dear children, without you I am not able to help the world.   I desire that you cooperate with me in everything, even in the smallest things.   Therefore, dear children, help me by letting your prayer be from the heart and all of you surrendering completely to me.   That way I shall be able to teach and lead you on this way which I have begun with you.   Thank you for having responded to my call."

DECEMBER 25, 1987

"Dear children! Rejoice with me! My heart is rejoicing because of Jesus and today I want to give Him to you. Dear children, I want each one of you to open your heart to Jesus and I will give Him to you with love. Dear children, I want Him to change you, to teach you and to protect you. Today I am praying in a special way for each one of you and I am presenting you to God so He will manifest Himself in you. I am calling you to sincere prayer with the heart so that every prayer of yours may be an encounter with God. In your work and in your everyday life, put God in the first place. I call you today with great seriousness to obey me and to do as I am calling you. Thank you for having responded to my call."

FEBRUARY 25, 1989

"Dear children! Today I invite you to prayer of the heart. Throughout this season of grace I wish each of you to be united with Jesus, but without unceasing prayer you cannot experience the beauty and greatness of the grace which God is offering you. Therefore, little children, at all times fill your heart with even the smallest prayers. I am with you and unceasingly keep watch over every heart which is given to me. Thank you for having responded to my call."

APRIL 25, 1991

"Dear children! Today I invite you all so that your prayer be prayer with the heart. Let each of you find time for prayer so that in prayer you discover God. I do not desire you to talk about prayer, but to pray. Let your every day be filled with prayer of gratitude to God for life and for all that you have. I do not desire your life to pass by in words but that you glorify God with deeds. I am with you and I am grateful to God for every moment spent with you. Thank you for having responded to my call."

MAY 25, 2003

"Dear children! Also today I call you to prayer. Renew your personal prayer, and in a special way pray to the Holy Spirit to help you pray with the heart. I intercede for all of you, little children, and call all of you to conversion. If you convert, all those around you will also be renewed and prayer will be a joy for them. Thank you for having responded to my call."

JULY 25, 2011

"Dear children! May this time be for you a time of prayer and silence. Rest your body and spirit, may they be in God's love. Permit me, little children, to lead you, open your hearts to the Holy Spirit so that all the good that is in you may blossom and bear fruit one hundred fold. Begin and end the day with prayer with the heart. Thank you for having responded to my call."

❧ CHAPTER 97 ❧
PREPARE FOR JESUS TO COME

NOVEMBER 25, 1993

"Dear children! I invite you in this time like never before to prepare for the coming of Jesus. Let little Jesus reign in your hearts and only then when Jesus is your friend will you be happy. It will not be difficult for you either to pray or offer sacrifices or to witness Jesus' greatness in your life because He will give you strength and joy in this time. I am close to you by my intercession and prayer and I love and bless all of you. Thank you for having responded to my call."

NOVEMBER 25, 2001

"Dear children! In this time of grace, I call you anew to prayer. Little children, pray and prepare your hearts for the coming of the King of Peace, that with His blessing He may give peace to the whole world. Peacelessness has begun to reign in hearts and hatred reigns in the world. That is why, you who live my messages be the light and extended hands to this faithless world that all may come to know the God of Love. Do not forget, little children, I am with you and bless you all. Thank you for having responded to my call."

❧ CHAPTER 98 ❧
PRIESTS, RELIGIOUS BROTHERS AND SISTERS

AUGUST 25, 1997

"Dear children! God gives me this time as a gift to you, so that I may instruct and lead you on the path of salvation. Dear children, now you do not comprehend this grace, but soon a time will come when you will lament for these messages. That is why, little children, live all of the words which I have given you through this time of grace and renew prayer, until prayer becomes a joy for you. Especially, I call all those who have consecrated themselves to my Immaculate Heart to become an example to others. I call all priests and religious brothers and sisters to pray the Rosary and to teach others to pray. The Rosary, little children, is especially dear to me. Through the Rosary open your heart to me and I am able to help you. Thank you for having responded to my call."

OCTOBER 2, 2006

"Dear children, I am coming to you in this your time, to direct the call to eternity to you. This is the call of love. I call you to love; because only through love will you come to know the love of God. Many think that they have faith in God and that they know his laws. They try to live according to them, but they do not do what is the most important; they do not love Him. My children, pray and fast. This is the way which will help you to open yourselves and to love. Only through the love of God is eternity gained. I am with you. I will lead you with the motherly love. Thank you for having responded." Our Lady added: "My children, priests' hands are blessed hands of my Son, respect them."

DECEMBER 2, 2006

"Dear children, in this joyful time of expectation of my Son, I desire that all the days of your earthly life may be a joyful expectation of my Son. I am calling you to holiness. I call you to be my apostles of holiness so that, through you, the Good News may illuminate all those whom you will meet. Fast and pray, and I will be with you. Thank you!"

ॐ CHAPTER 99 ॐ
PURIFICATION FROM SINS

DECEMBER 4, 1986

"Dear children! Today I call you to prepare your hearts for these days when the Lord particularly desires to purify you from all the sins of your past. You, dear children, are not able by yourselves, therefore I am here to help you. You pray, dear children! Only that way shall you be able to recognize all the evil that is in you and surrender it to the Lord so the Lord may completely purify your hearts. Therefore, dear children, pray without ceasing and prepare your hearts in penance and fasting. Thank you for having responded to my call."

JULY 2, 2011

"Dear children; today I call you to a difficult and painful step for your unity with my Son. I call you to complete admission and confession of sins, to purification. An impure heart cannot be in my Son and with my Son. An impure heart cannot give the fruit of love and unity. An impure heart cannot do correct and just things; it is not an example of the beauty of God's love to those who surround it and to those who have not come to know that love. You, my children, are gathering around me full of enthusiasm, desires and expectations, and I implore the Good Father to, through the Holy Spirit, put my Son - faith, into your purified hearts. My children, obey me, set out with me. As Our Lady was leaving, to her left she showed darkness and to her right a Cross in golden light."

ॐ CHAPTER 100 ॐ
PUT GOD IN FIRST PLACE

JANUARY 25, 1990

"Dear children! Today I invite you to decide for God once again and to choose Him before everything and above everything, so that He may work miracles in your life and that day by day your life may become joy with Him. Therefore, little children, pray and do not permit Satan to work in your life through misunderstandings, the non-understanding and non-acceptance of one another.   Pray that you may be able to comprehend the greatness and the beauty of the gift of life. Thank you for having responded to my call."

DECEMBER 25, 1991

"Dear children! Today in a special way I bring the little Jesus to you, that He may bless you with His blessing of peace and love. Dear children, do not forget that this is a grace which many people neither understand nor accept. Therefore, you who have said that you are mine, and seek my help, give all of yourself. First of all, give your love and example in your families. You say that Christmas is a family feast. Therefore, dear children, put God in the first place in your families, so that He may give you peace and may protect you not only from war, but also in peace protect you from every satanic attack. When God is with you, you have everything. But when you do not want Him, then you are miserable and lost, and you do not know on whose side you are. Therefore, dear children, decide for God. Then you will get everything. Thank you for having responded to my call."

MARCH 25, 1996

"Dear children! I invite you to decide again to love God above all else. In this time when due to the spirit of consumerism one forgets what it means to love and to cherish true values, I invite you again, little children, to put God in the first place in your life. Do not let Satan attract you through material things but, little children, decide for God who is freedom and love. Choose life and not death of the soul, little children, and in this time when you meditate upon the suffering and death of Jesus I invite you to decide for life which blossomed through the Resurrection, and that your life may be renewed today through conversion that shall lead you to eternal life. Thank you for having responded to my call."

JULY 25, 1996

"Dear children! Today I invite you to decide every day for God. Little children, you speak much about God, but you witness little with your life. Therefore, little children, decide for conversion, that your life may be true before God, so that in the truth of your life you witness the beauty God gave you. Little children, I invite you again to decide for prayer because through prayer, you will be able to live the conversion. Each one of you shall become in the simplicity, similar to a child which is open to the love of the Father. Thank you for having responded to my call."

DECEMBER 25, 1997

"Dear children! Also today I rejoice with you and I call you to the good. I desire that each of you reflect and carry peace in your heart and say: I want to put God in the first place in my life. In this way, little children, each of you will become holy. Little children, tell everyone, I want the good for you and he will respond with the good and, little children, good will come to dwell in the heart of each man. Little children, tonight I bring to you the good of my Son who gave His life to save you. That is why, little children, rejoice and extend your hands to Jesus who is only good. Thank you for having responded to my call."

NOVEMBER 25, 2000

"Dear children! Today when Heaven is near to you in a special way, I call you to prayer so that through prayer you place God in the first place. Little children, today I am near you and I bless each of you with my motherly blessing so that you have the strength and love for all the people you meet in your earthly life and that you can give God's love. I rejoice with you and I desire to tell you that your brother Slavko has been born into Heaven and intercedes for you. Thank you for having responded to my call."

FEBRUARY 25, 2005

"Dear children! Today I call you to be my extended hands in this world that puts God in the last place. You, little children, put God in the first place in your life. God will bless you and give you strength to bear witness to Him, the God of love and peace. I am with you and intercede for all of you. Little children, do not forget that I love you with a tender love. Thank you for having responded to my call."

DECEMBER 2, 2007

"Dear children! Today, while I am looking at your hearts, my heart is filled with pain and trepidation. My children, stop for a moment and look into your hearts. Is my Son, your God truly in the first place? Are His commandments truly the measure of your life? I am warning you again: without faith there is neither nearness of God nor the word of God which is the light of salvation and the light of common sense."

ॐ CHAPTER 101 ॐ
PUT PRAYER IN FIRST PLACE

MAY 25, 2002
"Dear children! Today I call you to put prayer in the first place in your life. Pray and may prayer, little children, be a joy for you. I am with you and intercede for all of you, and you, little children, be joyful carriers of my messages. May your life with me be joy. Thank you for having responded to my call."

ॐ CHAPTER 102 ॐ
READ HOLY SCRIPTURE

OCTOBER 18, 1984
"Dear children! Today I call on you to read the Bible every day in your homes and let it be in a visible place so as always to encourage you to read it and to pray. Thank you for having responded to my call."

AUGUST 25, 1996
"Dear children! Listen, because I wish to speak to you and to invite you to have more faith and trust in God, who loves you immeasurably. Little children, you do not know how to live in the grace of God, that is why I call you all anew, to carry the word of God in your heart and in thoughts. Little children, place the Sacred Scripture in a visible place in your family, and read and live it. Teach your children, because if you are not an example to them, children depart into Godlessness. Reflect and pray

and then God will be born in your heart and your heart will be joyous. Thank you for having for responded to my call."

APRIL 25, 2005
"Dear children! Also today, I call you to renew prayer in your families. By prayer and the reading of Sacred Scripture, may the Holy Spirit, who will renew you, enter into your families. In this way, you will become teachers of the faith in your family. By prayer and your love, the world will set out on a better way and love will begin to rule in the world. Thank you for having responded to my call."

JANUARY 25, 2006
"Dear children! Also today I call you to be carriers of the Gospel in your families. Do not forget, little children, to read Sacred Scripture. Put it in a visible place and witness with your life that you believe and live the Word of God. I am close to you with my love and intercede before my Son for each of you. Thank you for having responded to my call."

JANUARY 25, 2007
"Dear children! Put Sacred Scripture in a visible place in your family and read it. In this way, you will come to know prayer with the heart and your thoughts will be on God. Do not forget that you are passing like a flower in a field, which is visible from afar but disappears in a moment. Little children, leave a sign of goodness and love wherever you pass and God will bless you with an abundance of His blessing. Thank you for having responded to my call."

෨ CHAPTER 103 ෨
RENUNCIATION

SEPTEMBER 25, 1991
"Dear children! Today in a special way I invite you all to prayer and renunciation. For now as never before Satan wants to show the world his shameful face by which he wants to seduce as many people as possible onto the way of death and sin. Therefore, dear children, help my Immaculate Heart to triumph in the sinful world. I beseech all of you to

offer prayers and sacrifices for my intentions so I can present them to God for what is most necessary. Forget your desires, dear children, and pray for what God desires, and not for what you desire. Thank you for having responded to my call."

FEBRUARY 25, 1998

"Dear children! Also today I am with you and I, again, call all of you to come closer to me through your prayers. In a special way, I call you to renunciation in this time of grace. Little children, meditate on and live, through your little sacrifices, the passion and death of Jesus for each of you. Only if you come closer to Jesus will you comprehend the immeasurable love He has for each of you. Through prayer and your renunciation you will become more open to the gift of faith and love towards the Church and the people who are around you. I love you and bless you. Thank you for having responded to my call."

FEBRUARY 25, 2008

"Dear children! In this time of grace, I call you anew to prayer and renunciation. May your day be interwoven with little ardent prayers for all those who have not come to know God's love. Thank you for having responded to my call."

ൠ CHAPTER 104 ൟ
ROSARY

AUGUST 14, 1984 (TUESDAY)

This apparition was unexpected. Ivan was praying at home. After that he started to get ready to go to Church for the evening services. By surprise Our Lady appeared to him and told him to relate to the people. "I would like the people to pray along with me these days. And to pray as much as possible! And to fast strictly on Wednesdays and Fridays, and every day to pray at least one Rosary: the joyful, sorrowful and glorious mysteries." Our Lady asked that we accept this message with a firm will.

She especially requested this of the parishioners and the faithful of the surrounding places.

SEPTEMBER 27, 1984

"Dear children! You have helped me along by your prayers to realize my plans. Keep on praying that my plans be completely realized. I request the families of the parish to pray the family Rosary. Thank you for having responded to my call."

OCTOBER 8, 1984 (MONDAY)
(JAKOV WAS SICK AND RECEIVED THIS MESSAGE AT HOME.)

"Dear children, Let all the prayers you say in your homes in the evening be for the conversion of sinners because the world is in great sin. Every evening pray the Rosary."

JUNE 25, 1985 (TUESDAY)

"I invite you to call on everyone to pray the Rosary. With the Rosary you shall overcome all the adversities which Satan is trying to inflict on the Catholic Church. All you priests, pray the Rosary! Dedicate your time to the Rosary!" (This message Our Lady gave in response to the question of Marija Pavlovic: "Our Lady, what do you wish to recommend to priests?")

JUNE 12, 1986

"Dear children! Today I call you to begin to pray the Rosary with a living faith. That way I will be able to help you. You, dear children, wish to obtain graces, but you are not praying. I am not able to help you because you do not want to get started. Dear children, I am calling you to pray the Rosary and that your Rosary be an obligation which you shall fulfill with joy. That way you shall understand the reason I am with you this long. I desire to teach you to pray. Thank you for having responded to my call."

FEBRUARY 25, 1988

"Dear children! Today again I am calling you to prayer to complete surrender to God. You know that I love you and am coming here out of love so I could show you the path to peace and salvation for your souls. I want you to obey me and not permit Satan to seduce you. Dear children, Satan is very strong and, therefore, I ask you to dedicate your prayers to me so that those who are under his influence can be saved. Give witness by your life. Sacrifice your lives for the salvation of the world. I am with you, and I am grateful to you, but in heaven you shall receive the Father's reward which He has promised to you. Therefore, dear children, do not be afraid. If you pray, Satan cannot injure you even a little bit because you are God's children and He is watching over you. Pray and let the Rosary always be in your hand as a sign to Satan that you belong to me. Thank you for having responded to my call."

JANUARY 25, 1991

"Dear children! Today, like never before, I invite you to prayer. Let your prayer be a prayer for peace. Satan is strong and desires to destroy not only human life, but also nature and the planet on which you live. Therefore, dear children, pray that through prayer you can protect yourselves with God's blessing of peace. God has sent me among you so that I may help you. If you so wish, grasp for the Rosary. Even the Rosary alone can work miracles in the world and in your lives. I bless you and I remain with you for as long as it is God's will. Thank you for not betraying my presence here and I thank you because your response is serving the good and the peace."

AUGUST 25, 1997

"Dear children! God gives me this time as a gift to you, so that I may instruct and lead you on the path of salvation. Dear children, now you do not comprehend this grace, but soon a time will come when you will lament for these messages. That is why, little children, live all of the words which I have given you through this time of grace and renew prayer, until prayer becomes a joy for you. Especially, I call all those who have consecrated themselves to my Immaculate Heart to become an example to others. I call all priests and religious brothers and sisters to pray the Rosary and to teach others to pray. The Rosary, little children, is especially dear to me. Through the Rosary open your heart to me and I am able to help you. Thank you for having responded to my call."

❧ CHAPTER 105 ❧
SACRED HEART

APRIL 5, 1984

"Dear children! This evening I pray you especially to venerate the Heart of my Son, Jesus. Make reparation for the wound inflicted on the Heart of my Son. That Heart is offended by all kinds of sins. Thank you for coming this evening."

MARCH 25, 2009

"Dear children! In this time of spring, when everything is awakening from the winter sleep, you also awaken your souls with prayer so that they may be ready to receive the light of the risen Jesus. Little children, may He draw you closer to His Heart so that you may become open to eternal life. I pray for you and intercede before the Most High for your sincere conversion. Thank you for having responded to my call."

❧ CHAPTER 106 ❧
SATAN (SPIRITUAL WARFARE)

JULY 12, 1984

"Dear children! These days Satan wants to frustrate my plans. Pray that his plan not be realized. I will pray my Son Jesus to give you the grace to experience the victory of Jesus in the temptations of Satan. Thank you for having responded to my call."

JULY 19, 1984

"Dear children! These days you have been experiencing how Satan is working. I am always with you, and don't you be afraid of temptations because God is always watching over us. Also I have given myself to you and I sympathize with you even in the smallest temptation. Thank you for having responded to my call."

AUGUST 11, 1984 (SATURDAY)

"Dear children! Pray, because Satan wishes to complicate my plans still further. Pray with the heart and surrender yourselves to Jesus in prayer."

DECEMBER 27, 1984

"Dear children! This Christmas Satan wanted in a special way to spoil God's plans. You, dear children, have discerned Satan even on Christmas day itself. But God is winning in all your hearts. So let your hearts keep on being happy. Thank you for having responded to my call."

AUGUST 8, 1985

"Dear children! Today I call you especially now to advance against Satan by means of prayer. Satan wants to work still more now that you know he is at work. Dear children, put on the armor for battle and with the Rosary in your hand defeat him! Thank you for having responded to my call."

AUGUST 29, 1985

"Dear children! I am calling you to prayer! Especially since Satan wishes to take advantage of the yield of your vineyards. Pray that Satan does not succeed in his plan. Thank you for having responded to my call."

SEPTEMBER 5, 1985

"Dear children! Today I thank you for all the prayers. Keep on praying all the more so that Satan will be far away from this place. Dear children, Satan's plan has failed. Pray for fulfillment of what God plans in this parish. I especially thank the young people for the sacrifices they have offered up. Thank you for having responded to my call."

JANUARY 9, 1986

"Dear children! I call you by your prayers to help Jesus along in the fulfillment of all the plans which He is forming here. And offer your sacrifices to Jesus in order that everything is fulfilled the way He has planned it and that Satan can accomplish nothing. Thank you for having responded to my call."

JANUARY 30, 1986

"Dear children! Today I call you all to pray that God's plans for us may be realized and also everything that God desires through you! Help others to be converted, especially those who are coming to Medjugorje. Dear children, do not allow Satan to get control of your hearts, so you would be an image of Satan and not of me. I call you to pray for how you might be witnesses of my presence. Without you, God cannot bring to reality that which He desires. God has given a free will to everyone, and it's in your control. Thank you for having responded to my call."

AUGUST 7, 1986

"Dear children! You know that I promised you an oasis of peace, but you don't know that beside an oasis stands the desert, where Satan is lurking and wanting to tempt each one of you. Dear children, only by prayer are you able to overcome every influence of Satan in your place. I am with you, but I cannot take away your freedom. Thank you for having responded to my call."

SEPTEMBER 4, 1986

"Dear children! Today again I am calling you to prayer and fasting. You know, dear children, that with your help I am able to accomplish everything and force Satan not to be seducing to evil and to remove himself from this place. Dear children, Satan is lurking for each individual. Especially in everyday affairs he wants to spread confusion among each one of you. Therefore, dear children, my call to you is that your day would be only prayer and complete surrender to God. Thank you for having responded to my call."

SEPTEMBER 18, 1986

"Dear children! Today again I thank you for all that you have accomplished for me in these days. Especially, dear children, I thank you in the Name of Jesus for the sacrifices which you offered in this past week. Dear children, you are forgetting that I desire sacrifices from you so I can help you and drive Satan away from you. Therefore, I am calling you again to offer sacrifices with a special reverence toward God. Thank you for having responded to my call."

SEPTEMBER 25, 1986

"Dear children! By your own peace I am calling you to help others to see and begin to seek peace. You, dear children, are at peace and not able to comprehend lack of peace. Therefore, I am calling you, so that by your prayer and your life you help to destroy everything that is evil in people and uncover the deception that Satan makes use of. You pray that the truth prevails in all hearts. Thank you for having responded to my call."

OCTOBER 16, 1986

"Dear children! Today again I want to show you how much I love you, but I am sorry that I am not able to help each one to understand my love. Therefore, dear children, I am calling you to prayer and complete surrender to God, because Satan wants to sift you through everyday affairs and in your life he wants to snatch the first place. Therefore, dear children, pray without ceasing! Thank you for having responded to my call."

MAY 25, 1987

"Dear children! I am calling everyone of you to start living in God's love. Dear children, you are ready to commit sin, and to put yourselves in the hand of Satan without reflecting. I call on each one of you to consciously decide for God and against Satan. I am your Mother and, therefore, I want to lead you all to perfect holiness. I want each one of you to be happy here on earth and to be with me in Heaven. That is, dear children, the purpose of my coming here and it's my desire. Thank you for having responded to my call."

SEPTEMBER 25, 1987

"Dear children! Today also I want to call you all to prayer. Let prayer be your life. Dear children, dedicate your time only to Jesus and He will give you everything that you are seeking. He will reveal Himself to you in fullness. Dear children, Satan is strong and is waiting to test each one of you. Pray, and that way he will neither be able to injure you nor block you on the way of holiness. Dear children, through prayer grow all the more toward God from day to day. Thank you for having responded to my call."

NOVEMBER 25, 1989

"Dear children! I am inviting you for years by these messages which I am giving you. Little children, by means of the messages I wish to make a very beautiful mosaic in your hearts, so I may be able to present each one of you to God like the original image. Therefore, little children, I desire that your decisions be free before God, because He has given you freedom. Therefore pray, so that, free from any influence of Satan, we may decide only for God. I am praying for you before God and I am seeking your surrender to God. Thank you for responding to my call."

SEPTEMBER 25, 1990

"Dear children! I invite you to pray with the heart in order that your prayer may be a conversation with God. I desire each one of you to dedicate more time to God. Satan is strong and wants to destroy and deceive you in many ways. Therefore, dear children, pray every day that your life will be good for yourselves and for all those you meet. I am with you and I am protecting you even though Satan wishes to destroy my plans and to hinder the desires which the Heavenly Father wants to realize here. Thank you for having responded to my call."

DECEMBER 25, 1990

"Dear children! Today I invite you in a special way to pray for peace. Dear children, without peace you cannot experience the birth of the little Jesus neither today nor in your daily lives. Therefore, pray the Lord of Peace that He may protect you with His mantle and that He may help you to comprehend the greatness and the importance of peace in your heart. In this way you shall be able to spread peace from your heart throughout the whole world. I am with you and I intercede for you before God. Pray, because Satan wants to destroy my plans of peace. Be reconciled with one another and by means of your lives help peace reign in the whole earth. Thank you for having responded to my call."

JANUARY 25, 1991

"Dear children! Today, like never before, I invite you to prayer. Let your prayer be a prayer for peace. Satan is strong and desires to destroy not only human life, but also nature and the planet on which you live. Therefore, dear children, pray that through prayer you can protect yourselves with God's blessing of peace. God has sent me among you so that I may help you. If you so wish, grasp for the rosary. Even the Rosary alone can work miracles in the world and in your lives. I bless you and I remain with you for as long as it is God's will. Thank you for not betraying my presence here and I thank you because your response is serving the good and the peace."

AUGUST 25, 1991

"Dear Children! Today also I invite you to prayer, now as never before when my plan has begun to be realized. Satan is strong and wants to sweep away plans of peace and joy and make you think that my Son is not strong in his decisions. Therefore, I call all of you, dear children, to pray and fast still more firmly. I invite you to renunciation for nine days, so that with your help, everything I wanted to realize through the secrets I began in Fatima may be fulfilled. I call you, dear children, to grasp the importance of my coming and the seriousness of the situation. I want to save all souls and present them to God. Therefore, let us pray that everything I have begun be fully realized. Thank you for having responded to my call."

SEPTEMBER 25, 1991

"Dear children! Today in a special way I invite you all to prayer and renunciation. For now as never before Satan wants to show the world his shameful face by which he wants to seduce as many people as possible onto the way of death and sin. Therefore, dear children, help my Immaculate Heart to triumph in the sinful world. I beseech all of you to offer prayers and sacrifices for my intentions so I can present them to God for what is most necessary. Forget your desires, dear children, and pray for what God desires, and not for what you desire. Thank you for having responded to my call."

FEBRUARY 25, 1992

"Dear children! Today I invite you to draw still closer to God through prayer. Only that way will I be able to help you and to protect you from every attack of Satan. I am with you and I intercede for you with God, that He protect you. But I need your prayers and your - "Yes." You get lost easily in material and human things, and forget that God is your greatest friend. Therefore, my dear little children, draw close to God so He may protect you and guard you from every evil. Thank you for having responded to my call!"

MARCH 25, 1992

"Dear children! Today as never before I invite you to live my messages and to put them into practice in your life. I have come to you to help you and, therefore, I invite you to change your life because you have taken a path of misery, a path of ruin. When I told you: convert, pray, fast, be reconciled, you took these messages superficially. You started to live them and then you stopped, because it was difficult for you. No, dear children, when something is good, you have to persevere in the good and not think: God does not see me, He is not listening, He is not helping. And so you have gone away from God and from me because of your miserable interest. I wanted to create of you an oasis of peace, love and goodness. God wanted you, with your love and with His help, to do miracles and, thus, give an example. Therefore, here is what I say to you: Satan is playing with you and with your souls and I cannot help you because you are far away from my heart. Therefore, pray, live my messages and then you will see the miracles of God's love in your everyday life. Thank you for having responded to my call."

APRIL 25, 1992

"Dear children! Today also I invite you to prayer. Only by prayer and fasting can war be stopped. Therefore, my dear little children, pray and by your life give witness that you are mine and that you belong to me, because Satan wishes in these turbulent days to seduce as many souls as possible. Therefore, I invite you to decide for God and He will protect you and show you what you should do and which path to take. I invite all those who have said "yes" to me to renew their consecration to my Son Jesus and to His Heart and to me so we can take you more intensely as instruments of peace in this unpeaceful world. Medjugorje is a sign to all of you and a call to pray and live the days of grace that God is giving you. Therefore, dear children, accept the call to prayer with seriousness. I am with you and your suffering is also mine. Thank you for having responded to my call."

SEPTEMBER 25, 1992

"Dear children! Today again I would like to say to you that I am with you also in these troubled days during which Satan wishes to destroy all that my Son Jesus and I are building. He desires especially to destroy your souls. He wants to take you away as far as possible from the Christian life and from the commandments that the Church calls you to live. Satan wishes to destroy everything that is holy in you and around you. This is why, little children, pray, pray, pray to be able to grasp all that God is giving you through my coming. Thank you for having responded to my call."

OCTOBER 25, 1992

"Dear children! I invite you to prayer now when Satan is strong and wishes to make as many souls as possible his own. Pray, dear children, and have more trust in me because I am here in order to help you and to guide you on a new path toward a new life. Therefore, dear little children, listen and live what I tell you because it is important for you when I shall not be with you any longer that you remember my words and all that I told you. I call you to begin to change your life from the beginning and that you decide for conversion not with words but with your life. Thank you for having responded to my call."

DECEMBER 25, 1992

"Dear children! I desire to place all of you under my mantle and protect you from all satanic attacks. Today is a day of peace, but in the whole world there is a great lack of peace. That is why I call you all to build a new world of peace with me through prayer. This I cannot do without you, and this is why I call all of you with my motherly love and God will do the rest. So, open yourselves to God's plan and to His designs to be able to cooperate with Him for peace and for everything that is good. Do not forget that your life does not belong to you, but is a gift with which you must bring joy to others and lead them to eternal life. May the tenderness of the little Jesus always accompany you. Thank you for having responded to my call."

MARCH 25, 1993

"Dear children! Today like never I call you to pray for peace, for peace in your hearts, peace in your families and peace in the whole world, because Satan wants war, wants lack of peace, wants to destroy all which is good. Therefore, dear children, pray, pray, pray. Thank you for having responded to my call."

JANUARY 25, 1994

"Dear children! You are all my children. I love you. But, little children, you must not forget that without prayer you cannot be close to me. In these times Satan wants to create disorder in your hearts and in your families. Little children, do not give in. You should not allow him to lead you and your life. I love you and intercede before God for you. Little children, pray. Thank you for having responded to my call."

MARCH 25, 1995

"Dear Children! Today I invite you to live the peace in your hearts and families. There is no peace, little children, where there is no prayer and there is no love, where there is no faith. Therefore, little children, I invite you all, to decide again today for conversion. I am close to you and I invite you all, little children, into my embrace to help you, but you do not want and in this way, Satan is tempting you, and in the smallest thing, your faith disappears. This is why little children, pray and through prayer, you will have blessing and peace. Thank you for having responded to my call."

MAY 25, 1995

"Dear Children! I invite you, little children, to help me through your prayers so that as many hearts as possible come close to my Immaculate Heart. Satan is strong and with all his forces wants to bring closer the most people possible to himself and to sin. That is why he is on the prowl to snatch more every moment. I beg you, little children, pray and help me to help you. I am your mother and I love you and that is why I wish to help you. Thank you for having responded to my call."

MARCH 25, 1996

"Dear children! I invite you to decide again to love God above all else. In this time when due to the spirit of consumerism one forgets what it means to love and to cherish true values, I invite you again, little children, to put God in the first place in your life. Do not let Satan attract you through material things but, little children, decide for God who is freedom and love. Choose life and not death of the soul, little children, and in this time when you meditate upon the suffering and death of Jesus I invite you to decide for life which blossomed through the Resurrection, and that your life may be renewed today through conversion that shall lead you to eternal life. Thank you for having responded to my call."

SEPTEMBER 25, 2001

"Dear children! Also today I call you to prayer, especially today when Satan wants war and hatred. I call you anew, little children: pray and fast that God may give you peace. Witness peace to every heart and be carriers of peace in this world without peace. I am with you and intercede before God for each of you. And you do not be afraid because the one who prays is not afraid of evil and has no hatred in the heart. Thank you for having responded to my call."

❧ CHAPTER 107 ❦
SEE MY SON IN EVERYONE

AUGUST 2, 2006
"Dear children, In these peaceless times I am coming to you to show you the way to peace. I love with an immeasurable love and I desire for you to love each other and to see in everyone my Son – the immeasurable love. The way to peace leads solely and only through love. Give your hand to me, your mother, and permit me to lead you. I am the Queen of Peace. Thank you."

AUGUST 2, 2007
"Dear children! Today I look in your hearts and looking at them my heart seizes with pain. My children! I ask of you unconditional, pure love for God. You will know that you are on the right path when you will be on earth with your body and with your soul always with God. Through this unconditional and pure love you will see my Son in every person. You will feel unity in God. As a Mother I will be happy because I will have your holy and unified hearts. My children, I will have your salvation. Thank you."

JULY 2, 2010
"Dear children, my motherly call, which I direct to you today, is a call of truth and life. My Son, who is Life, loves you and knows you in truth. To come to know and to love yourself, you must come to know my Son; to come to know and to love others, you must see my Son in them. Therefore, my children, pray, pray, that you may comprehend and surrender with a spirit that is free, be completely transformed and, in this

way, may have the Kingdom of Heaven in your heart on earth. Thank you!"

❧ CHAPTER 108 ❧
SILENCE OF HEART - PRAYERS

JULY 25, 1998

"Dear children! Today, little children, I invite you, through prayer, to be with Jesus, so that through a personal experience of prayer you may be able to discover the beauty of God's creatures. You cannot speak or witness about prayer, if you do not pray. That is why, little children, in the silence of the heart, remain with Jesus, so that He may change and transform you with His love. This, little children, is a time of grace for you. Make good use of it for your personal conversion, because when you have God, you have everything. Thank you for having responded to my call."

MAY 25, 2007

"Dear children! Pray with me to the Holy Spirit for Him to lead you in the search of God's will on the way of your holiness. And you, who are far from prayer, convert and, in the silence of your heart, seek salvation for your soul and nurture it with prayer. I bless you all individually with my motherly blessing. Thank you for having responded to my call."

❧ CHAPTER 109 ❧
SINCERELY REPENT FOR YOUR SINS

MAY 2, 2010

"Dear children! Today, through me, the good Father calls you to, with your soul filled with love, set out on a spiritual visitation. Dear children, be filled with grace, sincerely repent for your sins and yearn for the good. Yearn also in the name of those who have not come to know the perfection of the good. You will be more pleasing to God. Thank you."

❧ CHAPTER 110 ❧
SINNERS

AUGUST 2, 1984
"Dear children! Today I am joyful and I thank you for your prayers. Pray still more these days for the conversion of sinners. Thank you for having responded to my call."

OCTOBER 8, 1984 (MONDAY)
(JAKOV WAS SICK AND RECEIVED THIS MESSAGE AT HOME.)
"Dear children, Let all the prayers you say in your homes in the evening be for the conversion of sinners because the world is in great sin. Every evening pray the Rosary."

❧ CHAPTER 111 ❧
MESSAGES FOR ST. JAMES PARISH

MARCH 1, 1984
"Dear children! I have chosen this parish in a special way and I wish to lead it. I am guarding it in love and I want everyone to be mine. Thank you for having responded tonight. I wish you always to be with me and my Son in ever greater numbers. I shall speak a message to you every Thursday."

MARCH 8, 1984
"Thank you for having responded to my call! Dear children, you in the parish, be converted. This is my other wish. That way all those who shall come here shall be able to convert."

MARCH 22, 1984

"Dear children! In a special way this evening I am calling you during Lent to honor the wounds of my Son, which He received from the sins of this parish. Unite yourselves with my prayers for the parish so that His sufferings may be bearable. Thank you for having responded to my call. Try to come in ever greater numbers."

APRIL 12, 1984

"Dear children! Today I beseech you to stop slandering and to pray for the unity of the parish, because I and my Son have a special plan for this parish. Thank you for having responded to my call."

APRIL 30, 1984 (MONDAY)

Marija asked Our Lady, "Dear Madonna, why didn't you give me a message for the parish on Thursday?" Our Lady replied, "I do not wish to force anyone to do that which he/she neither feels nor desires, even though I had special messages for the parish by which I wanted to awaken the faith of every believer. But only a really small number has accepted my Thursday messages. In the beginning there were quite a few. But it's become a routine affair for them. And now recently some are asking for the message out of curiosity, and not out of faith and devotion to my Son and me."

MAY 10, 1984

Many of the faithful felt shaken by the last message of Our Lady. Some had the feeling that Our Lady would not give any more messages to the parish, but this evening she said, "I am speaking to you and I wish to speak further. You just listen to my instructions!"

MAY 17, 1984

"Dear children! Today I am very happy because there are many who want to consecrate themselves to me. Thank you. You have not made a mistake. My Son, Jesus Christ, wishes to bestow on you special graces through me. My Son is happy because of your dedication. Thank you for having responded to my call."

JUNE 9, 1984 (SATURDAY)

"Dear children! Tomorrow night pray for the Spirit of Truth! Especially, you from the parish. Because you need the Spirit of Truth to be able to convey the messages just the way they are, neither adding anything to them, nor taking anything whatsoever way from them, but just the way I said them. Pray for the Holy Spirit to inspire you with the spirit of prayer, so you will pray more. I, your Mother, tell you that you are praying little. Thank you for having responded to my call."

JULY 26, 1984

"Dear children! Today also I wish to call you to persistent prayer and penance. Especially, let the young people of this parish be more active in their prayers. Thank you for having responded to my call."

AUGUST 14, 1984 (TUESDAY)

This apparition was unexpected. Ivan was praying at home. After that he started to get ready to go to church for the evening services. By surprise Our Lady appeared to him and told him to relate to the people. "I would like the people to pray along with me these days. And to pray as much as possible! And to fast strictly on Wednesdays and Fridays, and every day to pray at least one Rosary: the joyful, sorrowful and glorious mysteries." Our Lady asked that we accept this message with a firm will. She especially requested this of the parishioners and the faithful of the surrounding places.

AUGUST 16, 1984

"Dear children! I beseech you, especially those from this parish, to live my messages and convey them to others, to whomever you meet. Thank you for having responded to my call."

AUGUST 23, 1984

"Dear children! Pray, pray!" Marija said that She also invited the people, and especially the young people, to keep order during the Mass.

AUGUST 30, 1984

"Dear children! The cross was also in God's plan when you built it. These days, especially, go on the mountain and pray before the cross. I need your prayers. Thank you for having responded to my call."

SEPTEMBER 6, 1984

"Dear children! Without prayer there is no peace. Therefore I say to you, dear children, pray at the foot of the cross for peace. Thank you for having responded to my call."

SEPTEMBER 20, 1984

"Dear children! Today I call on you to begin fasting with the heart. There are many people who are fasting, but only because everyone else is fasting. It has become a custom, which no one wants to stop. I ask the parish to fast out of gratitude because God has allowed me to stay this long in this parish. Dear children, fast and pray with the heart. Thank you for having responded to my call."

OCTOBER 11, 1984

"Dear children! Thank you for dedicating all your hard work to God even now when He is testing you through the grape you are picking. Be assured, dear children, that He loves you and, therefore, He tests you. You just always offer up all your burdens to God and do not be anxious. Thank you for having responded to my call."

DECEMBER 13, 1984

"Dear children! You know that the season of joy is getting closer, but without love you will achieve nothing. So first of all, begin to love your own family, everyone in the parish, and then you'll be able to love and accept all who are coming over here. Now let these seven days be a week when you need to learn to love. Thank you for having responded to my call."

DECEMBER 20, 1984

"Dear children! Today I am inviting you to do something concrete for Jesus Christ. As a sign of dedication to Jesus I want each family of the parish to bring a single flower before that happy day. I want every member of the family to have a single flower by the crib so Jesus can come and see your dedication to Him! Thank you for having responded to my call."

JANUARY 10, 1985

"Dear children! Today I want to thank you for all your sacrifices, but special thanks to those who have become dear to my heart and come here gladly are enough parishioners who are not listening to the messages, but because of those who are in a special way close to my heart, because of them I am giving messages for the parish. And I will go on giving them because I love you and I want you to spread my messages with your heart. Thank you for having responded to my call."

JANUARY 14, 1985 (MONDAY)

"My dear children! Satan is so strong and with all his might wants to disturb my plans which I have begun with you. You pray, just pray and don't stop for a minute! I will pray to my Son for the realization of all the plans I have begun. Be patient and constant in your prayers. And don't let Satan discourage you. He is working hard in the world. Be on your guard!" (Message conveyed by Vicka from Our Lady.)

JANUARY 17, 1985

"Dear children! These days Satan is working underhandedly against this parish, and you, dear children, have fallen asleep in prayer, and only some are going to Mass. Withstand the days of temptation! Thank you for having responded to my call."

JANUARY 24, 1985

"Dear children! These days you have experienced God's sweetness through the renewals which have been in this parish. Satan wants to work still more fiercely to take away your joy from each one of you. By prayer you can completely disarm him and ensure your happiness. Thank you for having responded to my call."

FEBRUARY 7, 1985

"Dear children! These days Satan is manifesting himself in a special way in this parish. Pray, dear children, that God's plan is brought into effect and that every work of Satan ends up for the glory of God. I have stayed with you this long so I might help you along in your trials. Thank you for having responded to my call."

FEBRUARY 14, 1985

"Dear children! Today is the day when I give you a message for the parish, but the whole parish is not accepting the messages and is not living them. I am saddened and I want you, dear children, to listen to me and to live my messages. Every family must pray family prayer and read the Bible! Thank you for having responded to my call."

FEBRUARY 21, 1985

"Dear children! From day to day I have been inviting you to renewal and prayer in the parish, but you are not accepting it. Today I am calling you for the last time! Now it's Lent and you as a parish can turn to my messages during Lent out of love. If you do not do that, I do not wish to keep on giving messages. God is permitting me that. Thank you for having responded to my call."

FEBRUARY 28, 1985

"Dear children! Today I call you to live the word this week: 'I love God!' Dear children through love you will achieve everything and even what you think is impossible. God wants this parish to belong completely to Him. And that's what I want too. Thank you for having responded to my call."

MARCH 7, 1985

"Dear children! Today I call you to renew prayer in your families. Dear children, encourage the very young to prayer and the children to go to Holy Mass. Thank you for having responded to my call."

MARCH 14, 1985

"Dear children! In your life you have all experienced light and darkness. God grants to every person to recognize good and evil. I am calling you to the light, which you should carry to all the people who are in darkness. People who are in darkness daily come into your homes. Dear children, give them the light! Thank you for having responded to my call."

MARCH 21, 1985

"Dear children! I wish to keep on giving messages and therefore today I call you to live and accept my messages! Dear children, I love you and in a special way I have chosen this parish, one more dear to me than the others, in which I have gladly remained when the Almighty sent me. Therefore I call on you - accept me, dear children, that it might go well with you. Listen to my messages! Thank you for having responded to my call."

APRIL 4, 1985 (HOLY THURSDAY)

"Dear children! I thank you for having started to think more about God's glory in your hearts. Today is the day when I wished to stop giving the messages because some individuals did not accept me. The parish has been moved and I wish to keep on giving you messages as it has never been in history from the beginning of the world. Thank you for having responded to my call."

APRIL 5, 1985 (GOOD FRIDAY)

"You parishioners have a great and heavy cross, but don't be afraid to carry it. My Son is here Who will help you." (Message given through Ivanka)

APRIL 11, 1985

"Dear children! Today I wish to say to everyone in the parish to pray in a special way to the Holy Spirit for enlightenment. From today God wishes to test the parish in a special way in order that He might strengthen it in faith. Thank you for having responded to my call."

APRIL 18, 1985

"Dear children! Today I thank you for every opening of your hearts. Joy overtakes me for every heart that is opened to God especially from the parish. Rejoice with me! Pray all the prayers for the opening of sinful hearts. I desire that. God desires that through me. Thank you for having responded to my call."

APRIL 25, 1985

"Dear children! Today I wish to tell you to begin to work in your hearts as you are working in the fields. Work and change your hearts so that a new spirit from God can take its place in your hearts. Thank you for having responded to my call."

MAY 31, 1984 (ASCENSION THURSDAY)

There were many people present from abroad. Our Lady did not give a message for the parish. She told Marija that she would give a message on Saturday to be announced at the Sunday parish Mass.

MAY 2, 1985

"Dear children! Today I call you to prayer with the heart, and not just from habit. Some are coming but do not wish to move ahead in prayer. Therefore, I wish to warn you like a Mother: pray that prayer prevails in your hearts in every moment. Thank you for having responded to my call."

MAY 30, 1985

"Dear children! I call you again to prayer with the heart. Let prayer, dear children, be your every day food in a special way when your work in the fields is so wearing you out that you cannot pray with the heart. Pray, and then you shall overcome even every weariness. Prayer will be your joy and your rest. Thank you for having responded to my call."

JUNE 6, 1985

"Dear children! During these days people from all nations will be coming into the parish. And now I am calling you to love: love first of all your own household members, and then you will be able to accept and love all who are coming. Thank you for having responded to my call."

JUNE 13, 1985

"Dear children! Until the anniversary day I am calling you, the parish, to pray more and to let your prayer be a sign of surrender to God. Dear children, I know that your are all tired, but you don't know how to surrender yourselves to me. During these days surrender yourselves completely to me! Thank your for having responded to my call."

JUNE 25, 1985 (TUESDAY)

"I invite you to call on everyone to pray the Rosary. With the Rosary you shall overcome all the adversities which Satan is trying to inflict on the Catholic Church. All you priests, pray the Rosary! Dedicate your time to the Rosary!" (This message Our Lady gave in response to the question of Marija Pavlovic: "Our Lady, what do you wish to recommend to priests?")

JUNE 28, 1985 (FRIDAY)

"Dear children! Today I am giving you a message through which I desire to call you to humility. These days you have felt great joy because of all the people who have come and to whom you could tell your experiences with love. Now I invite you to continue in humility and with an open heart speak to all who are coming. Thank you for having responded to my message."

JULY 4, 1985

"Dear children! I thank you for every sacrifice you have offered. And now I urge you to offer every sacrifice with love. I wish you, the helpless ones, to begin helping with confidence and the Lord will keep on giving to you in confidence. Thank you for having responded to my call."

JULY 11, 1985

"Dear children! I love the parish and with my mantle I protect it from every work of Satan. Pray that Satan retreats from the parish and from every individual who comes into the parish. In that way you shall be able to hear every call of God and answer it with your life. Thank you for having responded to my call.

AUGUST 1, 1985

"Dear children! I wish to tell you that I have chosen this parish and that I am guarding it in my hands like a little flower that does not want to die. I call you to surrender to me so that I can keep on presenting you to God, fresh and without sin. Satan has taken part of the plan and wants to possess it. Pray that he does not succeed in that, because I wish you for myself so I can keep on giving you to God. Thank you for having responded to my call."

OCTOBER 10, 1985

"Dear children! I wish also today to call you to live the messages in the parish. Especially I wish to call the youth of the parish, who are dear to me. Dear children, if you live the messages, you are living the seed of holiness. I, as the Mother, wish to call you all to holiness so that you can bestow it on others. You are a mirror to others! Thank you for having responded to my call."

NOVEMBER 21, 1985

"Dear children! I want to tell you that this season is especially for you from the parish. When it is summer, you saw that you have a lot of work. Now you don't have work in the fields, work on your own self personally! Come to Mass because this is the season given to you. Dear children, there are enough of those who come regularly despite bad weather because they love me and wish to show their love in a special way. What I want from you is to show me your love by coming to Mass, and the Lord will reward you abundantly. Thank you for having responded to my call."

FEBRUARY 6, 1986

"Dear children! This parish, which I have chosen, is special and different from others. And I am giving great graces to all who pray with the heart. Dear children, I am giving the messages first of all to the residents of the parish, and then to all the others. First of all you must accept the messages, and then the others. You shall be answerable to me and my Son, Jesus. Thank you for having responded to my call."

MAY 29, 1986

"Dear children! Today my call to you is that in your life you live love toward God and neighbor. Without love, dear children, you can do nothing. Therefore, dear children, I am calling you to live in mutual love. Only in that way will you be able to love and accept both me and all those around you who are coming into your parish. Everyone will sense my love through you. Therefore, I beseech you, dear children, to start loving from today with an ardent love, the love with which I love you. Thank you for having responded to my call."

JUNE 26, 1986

"Dear children! God is allowing me along with Himself to bring about this oasis of peace. I wish to call on you to protect it and that the oasis always be unspoiled. There are those who by their carelessness are destroying the peace and the prayer. I am inviting you to give witness and by your own life to help to preserve the peace. Thank you for having responded to my call."

NOVEMBER 25, 1987

"Dear children! Today also I call each one of you to decide to surrender again everything completely to me. Only that way will I be able to present each of you to God. Dear children, you know that I love you immeasurably and that I desire each of you for myself, but God has given to all a freedom which I lovingly respect and humbly submit to. I desire, dear children, that you help so that everything God has planned in this parish shall be realized. If you do not pray, you shall not be able to recognize my love and the plans which God has for this parish and for each individual. Pray that Satan does not entice you with his pride and deceptive strength. I am with you and I want you to believe me, that I love you. Thank you for having responded to my call."

❧ CHAPTER 112 ❦
FR. SLAVKO HAS BEEN BORN INTO HEAVEN

NOVEMBER 25, 2000

"Dear children! Today when Heaven is near to you in a special way, I call you to prayer so that through prayer you place God in the first place. Little children, today I am near you and I bless each of you with my motherly blessing so that you have the strength and love for all the people you meet in your earthly life and that you can give God's love. I rejoice with you and I desire to tell you that your brother Slavko has been born into Heaven and intercedes for you. Thank you for having responded to my call."

❧ CHAPTER 113 ❦
SOULS IN PURGATORY

NOVEMBER 6, 1986

"Dear children! Today I wish to call you to pray daily for souls in purgatory. For every soul prayer and grace is necessary to reach God and the love of God. By doing this, dear children, you obtain new intercessors who will help you in life to realize that all the earthly things are not important for you, that only Heaven is that for which it is necessary to strive. Therefore, dear children, pray without ceasing that you may be able to help yourselves and the others to whom your prayers will bring joy. Thank you for having responded to my call."

❧ CHAPTER 114 ❦
SPECIAL MESSAGES

FEBRUARY 13, 1986

"Dear children! This Lent is a special incentive for you to change. Start from this moment. Turn off the television and renounce various things that are of no value. Dear children, I am calling you individually to conversion. This season is for you. Thank you for having responded to my call."

OCTOBER 30, 1986

"Dear children! Today again I desire to call you to take seriously and carry out the messages which I am giving you. Dear children, it is for your sake that I have stayed this long so I could help you to fulfill all the messages which I am giving you. Therefore, dear children, out of love for me carry out all the messages which I am giving you. Thank you for having responded to my call."

DECEMBER 25, 1986 (CHRISTMAS DAY)

"Dear children! Today also I give thanks to the Lord for all that He is doing for me, especially for this gift that I am able to be with you also today. Dear children, these are the days in which the Father grants special graces to all who open their hearts. I bless you and I desire that you too, dear children, become alive to the graces and place everything at God's disposal so that He may be glorified through you. My heart carefully follows your progress. Thank you for having responded to my call."

APRIL 25, 1987

"Dear children! Today also I am calling you to prayer. You know, dear children, that God grants special graces in prayer. Therefore, seek and pray in order that you may be able to comprehend all that I am giving here. I call you, dear children, to prayer with the heart. You know that without prayer you cannot comprehend all that God is planning through each one of you. Therefore, pray! I desire that through each one of you God's plan may be fulfilled, that all which God has planted in your heart may keep on growing. So pray that God's blessing may protect each one of you from all the evil that is threatening you. I bless you, dear children. Thank you for having responded to my call."

JANUARY 25, 1988

"Dear children! Today again I am calling you to complete conversion, which is difficult for those who have not chosen God. God can give you everything that you seek from Him. But you seek God only when sicknesses, problems and difficulties come to you and you think that God is far from you and is not listening and does not hear your prayers. No, dear children, that is not the truth. When you are far from God, you cannot receive graces because you do not seek them with a firm faith. Day by day, I am praying for you, and I want to draw you ever more near to God, but I cannot if you don't want it. Therefore, dear children put your life in God's hands. I bless you all. Thank you for having responded to my call."

JANUARY 25, 1991

"Dear children! Today, like never before, I invite you to prayer. Let your prayer be a prayer for peace. Satan is strong and desires to destroy not only human life, but also nature and the planet on which you live. Therefore, dear children, pray that through prayer you can protect yourselves with God's blessing of peace. God has sent me among you so that I may help you. If you so wish, grasp for the rosary. Even the rosary alone can work miracles in the world and in your lives. I bless you and I remain with you for as long as it is God's will. Thank you for not betraying my presence here and I thank you because your response is serving the good and the peace."

AUGUST 25, 1991

"Dear Children! Today also I invite you to prayer, now as never before when my plan has begun to be realized. Satan is strong and wants to sweep away plans of peace and joy and make you think that my Son is not strong in his decisions. Therefore, I call all of you, dear children to pray and fast still more firmly. I invite you to renunciation for nine days so that, with your help, everything I wanted to realize through the secrets I began in Fatima, may be fulfilled. I call you, dear children, to grasp the importance of my coming and the seriousness of the situation. I want to save all souls and present them to God. Therefore, let us pray that everything I have begun be fully realized. Thank you for having responded to my call."

JANUARY 25, 1993

"Dear children! Today I call you to accept and live my messages with seriousness. These days are the days when you need to decide for God, for peace and for the good. May every hatred and jealousy disappear from your life and your thoughts, and may there only dwell love for God and for your neighbor. Thus, and only thus shall you be able to discern the signs of the time. I am with you and I guide you into a new time, a time which God gives you as grace so that you may get to know him more. Thank you for having responded to my call."

MARCH 18, 2003

"Dear children! Particularly at this holy time of penance and prayer, I call you to make a choice. God gave you free will to choose life or death. Listen to my messages with the heart that you may become cognizant of what you are to do and how you will find the way to life. My children, without God you can do nothing; do not forget this even for a single moment. For, what are you and what will you be on earth, when you will return to it again. Do not anger God, but follow me to life. Thank you for being here."

MARCH 25, 2003

"Dear children! Also today I call you to pray for peace. Pray with the heart, little children, and do not lose hope because God loves His creatures. He desires to save you, one by one, through my coming here. I call you to the way of holiness. Pray, and in prayer you are open to God's will; in this way, in everything you do, you realize God's plan in you and through you. Thank you for having responded to my call."

OCTOBER 25, 2003

"Dear children! I call you anew to consecrate yourselves to my heart and the heart of my Son Jesus. I desire, little children, to lead you all on the way of conversion and holiness. Only in this way, through you, we can lead all the more souls on the way of salvation. Do not delay, little children, but say with all your heart: "I want to help Jesus and Mary that all the more brothers and sisters may come to know the way of holiness. In this way, you will feel the contentment of being friends of Jesus. Thank you for having responded to my call."

FEBRUARY 25, 2004

"Dear children! Also today, as never up to now, I call you to open your hearts to my messages. Little children, be those who draw souls to God and not those who distance them. I am with you and love you all with a special love. This is a time of penance and conversion. From the bottom of my heart, I call you to be mine with all your heart and then you will see that your God is great, because He will give you an abundance of blessings and peace. Thank you for having responded to my call."

JUNE 25, 2006

"Dear children! With great joy in my heart I thank you for all the prayers that, in these days, you offered for my intentions. Know, little children, that you will not regret it, neither you nor your children. God will reward you with great graces and you will merit eternal life. I am near you and thank all those who, through these years, have accepted my messages, have poured them into their life and decided for holiness and peace. Thank you for having responded to my call."

AUGUST 2, 2010

"Dear children! Today I call you, together with me, to begin to build the Kingdom of Heaven in your hearts; that you may forget that what is personal and – led by the example of my Son – think of what is of God. What does He desire of you? Do not permit Satan to open the paths of earthly happiness, the paths without my Son. My children, they are false and last a short while. My Son exists. I offer you eternal happiness and peace and unity with my Son, with God; I offer you the Kingdom of God. Thank you."

SEPTEMBER 2, 2011

"Dear children; With all my heart and soul full of faith and love in the Heavenly Father, I gave my Son to you and am giving Him to you anew. My Son has brought you, the people of the entire world, to know the only true God and His love. He has led you on the way of truth and made you brothers and sisters. Therefore, my children, do not wander, do not close your heart before that truth, hope and love. Everything around you is passing and everything is falling apart, only the glory of God remains. Therefore, renounce everything that distances you from the Lord. Adore Him alone, because He is the only true God. I am with you and I will remain with you. I am especially praying for the shepherds that they may be worthy representatives of my Son and may lead you with love on the way of truth. Thank you."

❧ CHAPTER 115 ❧
SUFFERING

MARCH 29, 1984

"Dear children! In a special way this evening I am calling you to perseverance in trials. Consider how the Almighty is still suffering today on account of your sins. So when sufferings come, offer them up as a sacrifice to God. Thank you for having responded to my call."

SEPTEMBER 11, 1986

"Dear children! For these days while you are joyfully celebrating the cross, I desire that your cross also would be a joy for you. Especially, dear children, pray that you may be able to accept sickness and suffering with love the way Jesus accepted them. Only that way shall I be able with joy to give out to you the graces and healings which Jesus is permitting me. Thank you for having responded to my call."

SEPTEMBER 25, 1996

"Dear children! Today I invite you to offer your crosses and suffering for my intentions. Little children, I am your mother and I wish to help you by seeking for you the grace from God. Little children, offer your sufferings as a gift to God so they become a most beautiful flower of joy. That is why, little children pray that you may understand that suffering can become joy and the cross the way of joy. Thank you for having for responded to my call."

MARCH 25, 2006

"Courage, little children! I decided to lead you on the way of holiness. Renounce sin and set out on the way of salvation, the way which my Son has chosen. Through each of your tribulations and sufferings God will find the way of joy for you. Therefore, little children, pray. We are close to you with our love. Thank you for having responded to my call."

❧ CHAPTER 116 ❦
SURRENDER TO GOD

JANUARY 2, 1986

"Dear children! I call you to decide completely for God. I beseech you, dear children, to surrender yourselves completely and you shall be able to live everything I am telling you. It shall not be difficult for you to surrender yourselves completely to God. Thank you for having responded to my call."

OCTOBER 16, 1986

"Dear children! Today again I want to show you how much I love you, but I am sorry that I am not able to help each one to understand my love. Therefore, dear children, I am calling you to prayer and complete surrender to God, because Satan wants to sift you through everyday affairs and in your life he wants to snatch the first place. Therefore, dear children, pray without ceasing! Thank you for having responded to my call."

NOVEMBER 20, 1986

"Dear children! Today also I am calling you to live and follow with a special love all the messages which I am giving you. Dear children, God does not want you lukewarm and undecided, but that you totally surrender to Him. You know that I love you and that out of love I long for you. Therefore, dear children, you also decide for love so that you will long for and daily experience God's love. Dear children, decide for love so that love prevails in all of you, but not human love, rather God's love. Thank you for having responded to my call."

FEBRUARY 25, 1988

"Dear children! Today again I am calling you to prayer to complete surrender to God. You know that I love you and am coming here out of love so I could show you the path to peace and salvation for your souls. I want you to obey me and not permit Satan to seduce you. Dear children, Satan is very strong and, therefore, I ask you to dedicate your prayers to me so that those who are under his influence can be saved. Give witness by your life. Sacrifice your lives for the salvation of the world. I am with you, and I am grateful to you, but in heaven you shall receive the Father's reward which He has promised to you. Therefore, dear children, do not be afraid. If you pray, Satan cannot injure you even a little bit because you are God's children and He is watching over you. Pray and let the Rosary always be in your hand as a sign to Satan that you belong to me. Thank you for having responded to my call."

MARCH 25, 1988

"Dear children! Today also I am inviting you to a complete surrender to God. Dear children, you are not conscious of how God loves you with such a great love because He permits me to be with you so I can instruct you and help you to find the way of peace. This way, however, you cannot discover if you do not pray. Therefore, dear children, forsake everything and consecrate your time to God and God will bestow gifts upon you and bless you. Little children, don't forget that your life is fleeting like a spring flower, which today is wondrously beautiful, but tomorrow has vanished. Therefore, pray in such a way that your prayer, your surrender to God, may become like a road sign. That way, your witness will not only have value for yourselves but for all eternity. Thank you for having responded to my call."

APRIL 25, 1988

"Dear children! God wants to make you holy. Therefore, through me He is inviting you to complete surrender. Let holy mass be your life. Understand that the church is God's palace, the place in which I gather you and want to show you the way to God. Come and pray. Neither look at others nor slander them, but rather, let your life be a testimony on the way of holiness. Churches deserve respect and are set apart as holy because God, who became man, dwells in them day and night. Therefore, little children, believe and pray that the Father increase your faith, and then ask for whatever you need. I am with you and I am rejoicing because of you conversion and I am protecting you with my motherly mantle. Thank you for having responded to my call."

MAY 25, 1988

"Dear children! I am inviting you to a complete surrender to God. Pray, little children, that Satan may not carry you about like the branches in the wind. Be strong in God. I desire that through you the whole world may get to know the God of joy. By your life bear witness for God's joy. Do not be anxious nor worried. God himself will help you and show you the way. I desire that you love all men with my love. Only in that way can love reign over the world. Little children, you are mine. I love you and want you to surrender to me so that I can lead you to God. Never cease praying so that Satan cannot take advantage of you. Pray for the knowledge that you are mine. I bless you with blessings of joy. Thank you for having responded to my call."

JUNE 25, 1988

"Dear children! I am calling you to that love which is loyal and pleasing to God. Little children, love bears everything bitter and difficult for the sake of Jesus who is love. Therefore, dear children, pray that God come to your aid, not however according to your desire, but according to His love. Surrender yourself to God so that He may heal you, console you and forgive everything inside you which is a hindrance on the way of love. In this way God can move your life, and you will grow in love. Dear children, glorify God with a hymn of love so that God's love may be able to grow in you day by day to its fullness. Thank you for having responded to my call."

JULY 25, 1988

"Dear children! Today I am calling you to a complete surrender to God. Everything you do and everything you possess give over to God so that He can take control in your life as the King of all that you possess. That way, through me, God can lead you into the depths of the spiritual life. Little children, do not be afraid, because I am with you even if you think there is no way out and that Satan is in control. I am bringing peace to you I am your mother, the Queen of Peace. I am blessing you with the blessings of joy so that for you God may be everything in your life. Thank you for having responded to my call."

MARCH 25, 1989

"Dear children! I am calling you to a complete surrender to God. I am calling you to great joy and peace which only God can give. I am with you and I intercede for you every day before God. I call you, little children, to listen to me and to live the messages that I am giving you. Already for years you are invited to holiness but you are still far away. I am blessing you. Thank you for having responded to my call."

APRIL 25, 1989

"Dear children! I am calling you to a complete surrender to God. Let everything that you possess be in the hands of God. Only in that way shall you have joy in your heart. Little children, rejoice in everything that you have. Give thanks to God because everything is God's gift to you. That way in your life you shall be able to give thanks for everything and discover God in everything even in the smallest flower. Thank you for having responded to my call."

MAY 25, 1989

"Dear children! I invite you now to be open to God. See, children, how nature is opening herself and is giving life and fruits. In the same way I invite you to live with God and to surrender completely to him. Children, I am with you and I want to introduce you continuously to the joy of life. I desire that everyone may discover the joy and love which can be found only in God and which only God can give. God doesn't want anything from you only your surrender. Therefore, children, decide seriously for God because everything else passes away. Only God doesn't pass away. Pray to be able to discover the greatness and joy of life which God gives you. Thank you for having responded to my call."

JULY 25, 1989

"Dear children! Today I am calling you to renew your hearts. Open yourselves to God and surrender to him all your difficulties and crosses so, God may turn everything into joy. Little children, you cannot open yourselves to God if you do not pray. Therefore, from today, decide to consecrate a time in the day only for an encounter with God in silence. In that way you will be able, with God, to witness my presence here. Little children, I do not wish to force you. Rather freely give God your time, like children of God. Thank you for having responded to my call."

NOVEMBER 25, 1989

"Dear children! I am inviting you for years by these messages which I am giving you. Little children, by means of the messages I wish to make a very beautiful mosaic in your hearts, so I may be able to present each one of you to God like the original image. Therefore, little children, I desire that your decisions be free before God, because He has given you freedom. Therefore pray, so that, free from any influence of Satan, we may decide only for God. I am praying for you before God and I am seeking your surrender to God. Thank you for responding to my call."

FEBRUARY 25, 1990

"Dear children! I invite you to surrender to God. In this season I especially want you to renounce all the things to which you are attached but which are hurting your spiritual life. Therefore, little children, decide completely for God, and do not allow Satan to come into your life through those things that hurt both you and your spiritual life. Little children, God is offering Himself to you in fullness, and you can discover and recognize Him only in prayer. Therefore make a decision for prayer. Thank you for having responded to call."

APRIL 25, 1998

"Dear children! Today I call you, through prayer, to open yourselves to God as a flower opens itself to the rays of the morning sun. Little children, do not be afraid. I am with you and I intercede before God for each of you so that your heart receives the gift of conversion. Only in this way, little children, will you comprehend the importance of grace in these times and God will become nearer to you. Thank you for having responded to my call."

MAY 25, 1999

"Dear children! Also today I call you to convert and to more firmly believe in God. Children, you seek peace and pray in different ways, but you have not yet given your hearts to God for Him to fill them with His love. So, I am with you to teach you and to bring you closer to the love of God. If you love God above all else, it will be easy for you to pray and to open your hearts to Him. Thank you for having responded to my call."

❧ CHAPTER 117 ❧
SURRENDER TO MARY

MAY 15, 1986

"Dear children! Today I call you to give me your heart so I can change it to be like mine. You are wondering, dear children, why you cannot respond to that which I am seeking from you. You are not able to because you have not given me your heart so I can change it. You are talking but you are not doing. I call on you to do everything that I am telling you. That way I will be with you. Thank you for having responded to my call."

AUGUST 28, 1986

"Dear children! My call is that in everything you would be an image for others, especially in prayer and witnessing. Dear children, without you I am not able to help the world. I desire that you cooperate with me in everything, even in the smallest things. Therefore, dear children, help me by letting your prayer be from the heart and all of you surrendering completely to me. That way I shall be able to teach and lead you on this way which I have begun with you. Thank you for having responded to my call."

MAY 25, 1988

"Dear children! I am inviting you to a complete surrender to God. Pray, little children, that Satan may not carry you about like the branches in the wind. Be strong in God. I desire that through you the whole world may get to know the God of joy. By your life bear witness for God's joy. Do not be anxious nor worried. God himself will help you and show you the way. I desire that you love all men with my love. Only in that way can love reign over the world. Little children, you are mine. I love you and want you to surrender to me so that I can lead you to God. Never cease praying so that Satan cannot take advantage of you. Pray for the knowledge that you are mine. I bless you with blessings of joy. Thank you for having responded to my call."

AUGUST 25, 1992

"Dear children! Today I desire to tell you that I love you. I love you with my maternal love and I invite you to open yourselves completely to me so that, through each one of you, I can convert and save this world which is full of sin and bad things. That is why, my dear little children, you should open yourselves completely to me so that I may carry you always further toward the marvelous love of God the Creator who reveals Himself to you from day to day. I am with you and I wish to reveal to you and show you the God who loves you. Thank you for having responded to my call."

MARCH 25, 1994

"Dear children! Today I rejoice with you and I invite you to open yourselves to me, and become an instrument in my hands for the salvation of the world. I desire, little children, that all of you who have felt the odor of holiness through these messages which I am giving you to carry, to carry it into this world, hungry for God and God's love. I thank you all for having responded in such a number and I bless you all with my motherly blessing. Thank you for having responded to my call."

OCTOBER 25, 1998

"Dear children! Today I call you to come closer to my Immaculate Heart. I call you to renew in your families the fervor of the first days when I called you to fasting, prayer and conversion. Little children, you accepted my messages with open hearts, although you did not know what prayer was. Today, I call you to open yourselves completely to me so that I may transform you and lead you to the heart of my son Jesus, so that He can fill you with His love. Only in this way, little children, will you find true peace - the peace that only God gives you. Thank you for having responded to my call."

FEBRUARY 25, 1999

"Dear children! Also today I am with you in a special way contemplating and living the passion of Jesus in my heart. Little children, open your hearts and give me everything that is in them: joys, sorrows and each, even the smallest, pain, that I may offer them to Jesus; so that with His immeasurable love, He may burn and transform your sorrows into the joy of His resurrection. That is why, I now call you in a special way, little children, for your hearts to open to prayer, so that through prayer you may become friends of Jesus. Thank you for having responded to my call."

CHAPTER 118

TURN OFF YOUR TELEVISION

FEBRUARY 13, 1986

"Dear children! This Lent is a special incentive for you to change. Start from this moment. Turn off the television and renounce various things that are of no value. Dear children, I am calling you individually to conversion. This season is for you. Thank you for having responded to my call."

CHAPTER 119

THANKSGIVING TO GOD

JANUARY 3, 1985

"Dear children! These days the Lord has bestowed upon you great graces. Let this week be one of thanksgiving for all the graces which God has granted you. Thank you for having responded to my call."

OCTOBER 3, 1985

"Dear children! I wish to tell you to thank God for all the graces which God has given you. For all the fruits thank the Lord and glorify him! Dear children, learn to give thanks in little things and then you will be able to give thanks also for the big things. Thank you for having responded to my call."

AUGUST 25, 1988

"Dear children! Today I invite you all to rejoice in the life which God gives you. Little children, rejoice in God, the Creator, because He has created you so wonderfully. Pray that your life be joyful thanksgiving which flows out of your heart like a river of joy. Little children, give thanks unceasingly for all that you possess, for each little gift which God has given you, so that a joyful blessing always comes down from God upon your life. Thank you for having responded to my call."

SEPTEMBER 25, 1989

"Dear children! Today I invite you to give thanks to God for all the gifts you have discovered in the course of your life and even for the least gift that you have perceived. I give thanks with you and want all of you to experience the joy of these gifts. And I want God to be everything for each one of you. And then, little children, you can grow continuously on the way of holiness. Thank you for responding to my call."

OCTOBER 25, 1995

"Dear Children! Today I invite you to go into nature because there you will meet God the Creator. Today I invite you, little children, to thank

God for all that He gives you. In thanking Him you will discover the Most High and all the goods that surround you. Little children, God is great and His love for every creature is great. Therefore, pray to be able to understand the love and goodness of God. In the goodness and the love of God the Creator, I also am with you as a gift. Thank you for having responded to my call."

JULY 25, 1999

"Dear children! Also today I rejoice with you and I call you all to prayer with the heart. I call all of you, little children, to give thanks to God here with me for the graces which He gives to you through me. I desire for you to comprehend that I want to realize here, not only a place of prayer but also a meeting of hearts. I desire for my, Jesus' and your heart to become one heart of love and peace. That is why, little children, pray and rejoice over everything that God does here, despite that Satan provokes quarrels and unrest. I am with you and I lead you all on the way of love. Thank you for having responded to my call."

DECEMBER 25, 2000

"Dear children! Today when God granted to me that I can be with you, with little Jesus in my arms, I rejoice with you and I give thanks to God for everything He has done in this Jubilee year. I thank God especially for all the vocations of those who said 'yes' to God completely. I bless you all with my blessing and the blessing of the newborn Jesus. I pray for all of you for joy to be born in your hearts so that in joy you too carry the joy I have today. In this Child I bring to you the Savior of the your hearts and the One who calls you to the holiness of life. Thank you for having responded to my call."

AUGUST 25, 2003

"Dear children! Also today I call you to give thanks to God in your heart for all the graces which He gives you, also through the signs and colors that are in nature. God wants to draw you closer to Himself and moves you to give Him glory and thanks. Therefore, little children, I call you anew to pray, pray, pray and do not forget that I am with you. I intercede before God for each of you until your joy in Him is complete. Thank you for having responded to my call."

SEPTEMBER 25, 2004

"Dear children! Also today, I call you to be love where there is hatred and food where there is hunger. Open your hearts, little children, and let your hands be extended and generous so that, through you, every creature may thank God the Creator. Pray, little children, and open your heart to God's love, but you cannot if you do not pray. Therefore, pray, pray, pray. Thank you for having responded to my call."

AUGUST 25, 2006

"Dear children! Also today I call you to pray, pray, pray. Only in prayer will you be near to me and my Son and you will see how short this life is. In your heart a desire for Heaven will be born. Joy will begin to rule in your heart and prayer will begin to flow like a river. In your words there will only be thanksgiving to God for having created you and the desire for holiness will become a reality for you. Thank you for having responded to my call."

☙ CHAPTER 120 ❧
THE CROSS

SEPTEMBER 12, 1985

"Dear children! I wish to tell you that the cross should be central these days. Pray especially before the cross from which great graces are coming. Now in your homes make a special consecration to the cross. Promise that you will neither offend Jesus nor abuse the cross. Thank you for having responded to my call."

FEBRUARY 20, 1986

"Dear children! The second message of these Lenten days is that you renew prayer before the cross. Dear children, I am giving you special graces and Jesus is giving you special gifts from the cross. Take them and live! Reflect on Jesus' Passion and in your life be united with Jesus! Thank you for having responded to my call."

MARCH 25, 1997

"Dear children! Today, in a special way, I invite you to take the cross in the hands and to meditate on the wounds of Jesus. Ask of Jesus to heal your wounds, which you, dear children, during your life sustained because of your sins or the sins of your parents. Only in this way, dear children, you will understand that the world is in need of healing of faith in God the Creator. By Jesus' passion and death on the cross, you will understand that only through prayer you, too, can become true apostles of faith; when, in simplicity and prayer, you live faith which is a gift. Thank you for having responded to my call."

NOVEMBER 25, 2007

"Dear children! Today, when you celebrate Christ, the King of all that is created, I desire for Him to be the King of your lives. Only through giving, little children, can you comprehend the gift of Jesus´ sacrifice on the Cross for each of you. Little children, give time to God that He may transform you and fill you with His grace, so that you may be a grace for others. For you, little children, I am a gift of grace and love, which comes from God for this peaceless world. Thank you for having responded to my call."

❧ CHAPTER 121 ☙
THE SIGNS OF THE TIMES

APRIL 2, 2006

"Dear Children, I am coming to you, because, with my own example, I wish to show you the importance of prayer for those who have not come to know the love of God. You ask yourself if you are following me? My children, do you not recognize the signs of the times? Do you not speak of them? Come follow me. As a mother I call you. Thank you for having responded."

JUNE 2, 2007

"Dear children! Also in this difficult time God's love sends me to you. My children, do not be afraid, I am with you. With complete trust give me your hearts, that I may help you to recognize the signs of the time in which you live. I will help you to come to know the love of my Son. I will triumph through you. Thank you."

MAY 2, 2009

"Dear children! Already for a long time I am giving you my motherly heart and offering my Son to you. You are rejecting me. You are permitting sin to overcome you more and more. You are permitting it to master you and to take away your power of discernment. My poor children, look around you and look at the signs of the times. Do you think that you can do without God's blessing? Do not permit darkness to envelop you. From the depth of your heart cry out for my Son. His Name disperses even the greatest darkness. I will be with you, you just call me: 'Here we are Mother, lead us.' Thank you."

ॐ CHAPTER 122 ॐ
THE WAY OF SALVATION

OCTOBER 25, 2007

"Dear children! God sent me among you out of love that I may lead you towards the way of salvation. Many of you opened your hearts and accepted my messages, but many have become lost on this way and have never come to know the God of love with the fullness of heart. Therefore, I call you to be love and light where there is darkness and sin. I am with you and bless you all. Thank you for having responded to my call."

❧ CHAPTER 123 ❧
THESE ARE SPECIAL TIMES

JUNE 25, 1993
"Dear children! Today I also rejoice at your presence here. I bless you with my motherly blessing and intercede for each one of you before God. I call you anew to live my messages and to put them into life and practice. I am with you and bless all of you day by day. Dear children, these are special times and, therefore, I am with you to love and protect you; to protect your hearts from Satan and to bring you all closer to the heart of my Son, Jesus. Thank you for having responded to my call."

AUGUST 25, 1993
"Dear children! I want you to understand that I am your Mother, that I want to help you and call you to prayer. Only by prayer can you understand and accept my messages and practice them in your life. Read Sacred Scripture, live it, and pray to understand the signs of the times. This is a special time, therefore, I am with you to draw you close to my heart and the heart of my Son, Jesus. Dear little children, I want you to be children of the light and not of the darkness. Therefore, live what I am telling you. Thank you for having responded to my call."

❧ CHAPTER 124 ❧
THIS IS A NEW TIME

JANUARY 25, 1993
"Dear children! Today I call you to accept and live my messages with seriousness. These days are the days when you need to decide for God, for peace and for the good. May every hatred and jealousy disappear from your life and your thoughts, and may there only dwell love for God and for your neighbor. Thus, and only thus shall you be able to discern the signs of the time. I am with you and I guide you into a new time, a time which God gives you as grace so that you may get to know him more. Thank you for having responded to my call."

OCTOBER 25, 2000

"Dear children! Today I desire to open my motherly heart to you and to call you all to pray for my intentions. I desire to renew prayer with you and to call you to fast which I desire to offer to my Son Jesus for the coming of a new time; a time of spring. In this Jubilee year many hearts have opened to me and the Church is being renewed in the Spirit. I rejoice with you and I thank God for this gift; and you, little children, I call to pray, pray, pray, until prayer becomes a joy for you. Thank you for having responded to my call."

❧ CHAPTER 125 ❧
THIS IS THE TIME OF GRACE

DECEMBER 25, 1995

"Dear Children! Today I also rejoice with you and I bring you little Jesus, so that He may bless you. I invite you, dear children, so that your life may be united with Him. Jesus is the King of Peace and only He can give you the peace that you seek. I am with you and I present you to Jesus in a special way, now in this new time in which one should decide for Him. This time is the time of grace. Thank you for having responded to my call."

OCTOBER 25, 1999

"Dear children! Do not forget: this is a time of grace; that is why, pray, pray, pray! Thank you for having responded to my call."

MARCH 25, 2000

"Dear children! Pray and make good use of this time, because this is a time of grace. I am with you and I intercede for each one of you before God, for your heart to open to God and to God's love. Little children, pray without ceasing, until prayer becomes a joy for you. Thank you for having responded to my call."

FEBRUARY 25, 2001

"Dear children! This is a time of grace. That is why pray, pray, pray until you comprehend God's love for each of you. Thank you for having responded to my call."

MARCH 25, 2001

"Dear children! Also today I call you to open yourselves to prayer. Little children, you live in a time in which God gives great graces but you do not know how to make good use of them. You are concerned about everything else, but the least for the soul and spiritual life. Awaken from the tired sleep of your soul and say yes to God with all your strength. Decide for conversion and holiness. I am with you, little children, and I call you to perfection of your soul and of everything you do. Thank you for having responded to my call."

DECEMBER 25, 2002

"Dear children! This is a time of great graces, but also a time of great trials for all those who desire to follow the way of peace. Because of that, little children, again I call you to pray, pray, pray, not with words but with the heart. Live my messages and be converted. Be conscious of this gift that God has permitted me to be with you, especially today when in my arms I have little Jesus - the King of Peace. I desire to give you peace, and that you carry it in your hearts and give it to others until God's peace begins to rule the world. Thank you for having responded to my call."

AUGUST 25, 2005

"Dear Children! Also today I call you to live my messages. God gave you a gift of this time as a time of grace. Therefore, little children, make good use of every moment and pray, pray, pray. I bless you all and intercede before the Most High for each of you. Thank you for having responded to my call."

OCTOBER 25, 2006

"Dear children! Today the Lord permitted me to tell you again that you live in a time of grace. You are not conscious, little children, that God is giving you a great opportunity to convert and to live in peace and love. You are so blind and attached to earthly things and think of earthly life. God sent me to lead you toward eternal life. I, little children, am not tired, although I see that your hearts are heavy and tired for everything that is a grace and a gift. Thank you for having responded to my call."

APRIL 25, 2007

"Dear children! Also today I again call you to conversion. Open your hearts. This is a time of grace while I am with you, make good use of it. Say: 'This is the time for my soul.' I am with you and love you with immeasurable love. Thank you for having responded to my call."

NOVEMBER 25, 2011

"Dear children! Today I desire to give you hope and joy. Everything that is around you, little children, leads you towards worldly things but I desire to lead you towards a time of grace, so that through this time you may be all the closer to my Son, that He can lead you towards His love and eternal life, for which every heart yearns. You, little children, pray and may this time for you be one of grace for your soul. Thank you for having responded to my call."

❧ CHAPTER 126 ❧
THIS TIME IS MY TIME

JANUARY 25, 1997

"Dear children! I invite you to reflect about your future. You are creating a new world without God, only with your own strength and that is why you are unsatisfied and without joy in the heart. This time is my time and that is why, little children, I invite you again to pray. When you find unity with God, you will feel hunger for the word of God and your heart, little children, will overflow with joy. You will witness God's love wherever you are. I bless you and I repeat to you that I am with you to help you. Thank you for having responded to my call."

❧ CHAPTER 127 ❧
TRIALS SENT BY GOD

AUGUST 22, 1985

"Dear children! Today I wish to tell you that God wants to send you trials which you can overcome by prayer. God is testing you through daily chores. Now pray to peacefully withstand every trial. From everything through which God tests you come out more open to God and approach Him with love. Thank you for having responded to my call."

❧ CHAPTER 128 ❧
VALUE OF PRAYER

OCTOBER 2, 1986

"Dear children! Today again I am calling you to pray. You, dear children, are not able to understand how great the value of prayer is as long as you yourselves do not say: 'now is the time for prayer, now nothing else is important to me, now not one person is important to me but God.' Dear children, consecrate yourselves to prayer with a special love so that God will be able to render graces back to you. Thank you for having responded to my call."

❧ CHAPTER 129 ❧
WHAT IS THE MOST IMPORTANT TO YOUR SOUL

DECEMBER 2, 2009

"Dear children! At this time of preparation and joyful expectation I, as a mother, desire to point you to what is the most important to your soul. Can my Son be born in it? Is it cleansed by love from lies, arrogance, hatred and malice? Above all else does your soul love God as your Father and does it love your fellow brother in Christ? I am pointing you to the way which will raise your soul to a complete union with my Son. I desire for my Son to be born in you. What a joy that would be for me as mother. Thank you."

❧ CHAPTER 130 ❧
WITH AN OPEN HEART

JUNE 28, 1985 (FRIDAY)
"Dear children! Today I am giving you a message through which I desire to call you to humility. These days you have felt great joy because of all the people who have come and to whom you could tell your experiences with love. Now I invite you to continue in humility and with an open heart speak to all who are coming. Thank you for having responded to my message."

DECEMBER 25, 2000
"Dear children! Today when Jesus is born and by His birth brings immeasurable joy, love and peace, I call you, in a special way to say your yes to Jesus. Open your hearts so that Jesus enters into them, comes to dwell in them and starts to work through you. Only in this way will you be able to comprehend the true beauty of God's love, joy and peace. Dear children, rejoice in the birth of Jesus and pray for all those hearts that have not opened to Jesus so that Jesus may enter into each of their hearts and may start working through them, so that every person would be an example of a true person through whom God works."

MARCH 25, 2002
"Dear children! Today I call you to unite with Jesus in prayer. Open your heart to Him and give Him everything that is in it: joys, sorrows and illnesses. May this be a time of grace for you. Pray, little children, and may every moment belong to Jesus. I am with you and I intercede for you. Thank you for having responded to my call."

OCTOBER 25, 2005

"Little children, believe, pray and love, and God will be near you. He will give you the gift of all the graces you seek from Him. I am a gift to you, because, from day to day, God permits me to be with you and to love each of you with immeasurable love. Therefore, little children, in prayer and humility, open your hearts and be witnesses of my presence. Thank you for having responded to my call."

MAY 2, 2006

"Dear Children, I am coming to you as a mother. I am coming with an open heart full of love for you, my children. Cleanse your hearts from everything that prevents you from receiving me; from recognizing the love of my Son. Through you, my heart desires to win – desires to triumph. Open your hearts; I will lead you to this. Thank you!"

FEBRUARY 25, 2006

"Dear children! In this Lenten time of grace, I call you to open your hearts to the gifts that God desires to give you. Do not be closed, but with prayer and renunciation say 'yes' to God and He will give to you in abundance. As in springtime the earth opens to the seed and yields a hundredfold, so also your heavenly Father will give to you in abundance. I am with you and love you, little children, with a tender love. Thank you for having responded to my call."

MAY 2, 2008

"Dear children! By God's will I am here with you in this place. I desire for you to open your hearts to me and to accept me as a mother. With my love I will teach you simplicity of life and richness of mercy and I will lead you to my Son. The way to Him can be difficult and painful but do not be afraid, I will be with you. My hands will hold you to the very end, to the eternal joy; therefore do not be afraid to open yourselves to me. Thank you."

NOVEMBER 2, 2008

"Dear children, today I call you to a complete union with God. Your body is on earth, but I ask you for your soul to be all the more often in God's nearness. You will achieve this through prayer, prayer with an open heart. In that way you will thank God for the immeasurable goodness which He gives to you through me and, with a sincere heart, you will receive the obligation to treat the souls whom you meet with equal goodness. Thank you, my children."

NOVEMBER 25, 2010

"Dear children! I look at you and I see in your heart death without hope, restlessness and hunger. There is no prayer or trust in God, that is why the Most High permits me to bring you hope and joy. Open yourselves. Open your hearts to God's mercy and He will give you everything you need and will fill your hearts with peace, because He is peace and your hope. Thank you for having responded to my call."

DECEMBER 2, 2010

"Dear children! Today I am praying here with you that you may gather the strength to open your hearts and thus to become aware of the mighty love of the suffering God. Through this His love, goodness and meekness, I am also with you. I invite you for this special time of preparation to be a time of prayer, penance and conversion. My children, you need God. You cannot go forward without my Son. When you comprehend and accept this, what was promised to you will be realized. Through the Holy Spirit the Kingdom of Heaven will be born in your hearts. I am leading you to this. Thank you."

❧ CHAPTER 131 ❧
WITH MY SON, YOU CAN HEAL THE WORLD

AUGUST 2, 2011

"Dear children; Today I call you to be born anew in prayer and through the Holy Spirit, to become a new people with my Son; a people who knows that if they have lost God, they have lost themselves; a people who knows that, with God, despite all sufferings and trials, they are secure and saved. I call you to gather into God's family and to be strengthened with the Father's strength. As individuals, my children, you cannot stop the evil that wants to begin to rule in this world and to destroy it. But, according to God's will, all together, with my Son, you can change everything and heal the world. I call you to pray with all your heart for your shepherds, because my Son chose them. Thank you."

❧ CHAPTER 132 ⷶ
WITHOUT JESUS YOU DO NOT HAVE JOY AND PEACE, NOR A FUTURE OR ETERNAL LIFE

JULY 25, 2010

"Dear children! Anew I call you to follow me with joy. I desire to lead all of you to my Son, your Savior. You are not aware that without Him you do not have joy and peace, nor a future or eternal life. Therefore, little children, make good use of this time of joyful prayer and surrender. Thank you for having responded to my call."

❧ CHAPTER 133 ⷶ
WITNESS LOVE IN THE NAME OF MY SON

JUNE 2, 2009

"Dear children! My love seeks your complete and unconditional love, which will not leave you the same as you are, instead it will change you and teach you to trust in my Son. My children, with my love I am saving you and making you true witnesses of the goodness of my Son. Therefore, my children, do not be afraid to witness love in the name of my Son. Thank you."

❧ CHAPTER 134 ⷶ
WORK IN CHURCH / WORKS OF MERCY

OCTOBER 31, 1985

"Dear children! Today I wish to call you to work in the Church. I love all the same and I desire from each one to work as much as is possible. I know, dear children, that you can, but you do not wish to because you feel small and humble in these things. You need to be courageous and with little flowers do your share for the church and for Jesus so that everyone can be satisfied. Thank you for having responded to my call."

MARCH 25, 1987

"Dear children! Today I am grateful to you for your presence in this place, where I am giving you special graces. I call each one of you to begin to live as of today that life which God wishes of you and to begin to perform good works of love and mercy. I do not want you, dear children, to live the message and be committing sin which is displeasing to me. Therefore, dear children, I want each of you to live a new life without destroying all that God produces in you and is giving you. I give you my special blessing and I am remaining with you on your way of conversion. Thank you for having responded to my call."

NOVEMBER 25, 1990

"Dear children! Today I invite you to do works of mercy with love and out of love for me and for your and my brothers and sisters. Dear children, all that you do for others, do it with great joy and humility towards God. I am with you and day after day I offer your sacrifices and prayers to God for the salvation of the world. Thank you for having responded to my call."

FEBRUARY 25, 1993

"Dear children! Today I bless you with my motherly blessing and I invite you all to conversion. I wish that each of you decide for a change of life and that each of you works more in the Church not through words and thoughts but through example, so that your life may be a joyful testimony for Jesus. You cannot say that you are converted, because your life must become a daily conversion. In order to understand what you have to do, little children, pray and God will give you what you completely have to do, and where you have to change. I am with you and place you all under my mantle. Thank you for having responded to my call."

↘ CHAPTER 135 ↙
WORK ON SALVATION OF THE WORLD

MAY 25, 2008

"Dear children! In this time of grace, when God has permitted me to be with you, little children, I call you anew to conversion. Work on the salvation of the world in a special way while I am with you. God is merciful and gives special graces, therefore, seek them through prayer. I am with you and do not leave you alone. Thank you for having responded to my call."

↘ CHAPTER 136 ↙
YOU ARE FORGETTING TO PRAY PROPERLY

FEBRUARY 2, 2011

"Dear children; You are gathering around me, you are seeking your way, you are seeking, you are seeking the truth but are forgetting what is the most important, you are forgetting to pray properly. Your lips pronounce countless words, but your spirit does not feel anything. Wandering in darkness, you even imagine God Himself according to yourselves, and not such as He really is in His love. Dear children, proper prayer comes from the depth of your heart, from your suffering, from your joy, from your seeking the forgiveness of sins. This is the way to come to know the right God and by that also yourselves, because you are created according to Him. Prayer will bring you to the fulfillment of my desire, of my mission here with you, to the unity in God's family. Thank you." Our Lady blessed everyone present, thanked them and called us to pray for priests."

❧ CHAPTER 137 ❧
YOU ARE GOD'S FAMILY

JANUARY 2, 2011

"Dear children; Today I call you to unity in Jesus, my Son. My motherly heart prays that you may comprehend that you are God's family. Through the spiritual freedom of will, which the Heavenly Father has given you, you are called to become cognizant (to come to the knowledge) of the truth, the good or the evil. May prayer and fasting open your hearts and help you to discover the Heavenly Father through my Son. In discovering the Father, your life will be directed to carrying out of God's will and the realization of God's family, in the way that my Son desires. I will not leave you alone on this path. Thank you."

❧ CHAPTER 138 ❧
YOU ARE NOT RESPONDING TO MY CALLS

FEBRUARY 2, 2009

"Dear children! With a motherly heart, today I desire to remind you of, namely, to draw your attention to, God's immeasurable love and the patience which ensues from it. Your Father is sending me and is waiting. He is waiting for your open hearts to be ready for His works. He is waiting for your hearts to be united in Christian love and mercy in the spirit of my Son. Do not lose time, children, because you are not its masters. Thank you."

APRIL 2, 2009

"Dear children! God's love is in my words. My children, that is the love which desires to turn you to justice and truth. That is the love which desires to save you from delusion. And what about you, my children? Your hearts remain closed; they are hard and do not respond to my calls. They are insincere. With a motherly love I am praying for you, because I desire for all of you to resurrect in my Son. Thank you."

੭ CHAPTER 139 ୭

YOU ARE PERMITTING SIN TO MASTER YOU

MAY 2, 2009

Our Lady was very sad. She only gave a message and blessed us.

"Dear children! Already for a long time I am giving you my motherly heart and offering my Son to you. You are rejecting me. You are permitting sin to overcome you more and more. You are permitting it to master you and to take away your power of discernment. My poor children, look around you and look at the signs of the times. Do you think that you can do without God's blessing? Do not permit darkness to envelop you. From the depth of your heart cry out for my Son. His Name disperses even the greatest darkness. I will be with you, you just call me: 'Here we are Mother, lead us.' Thank you."

੭ CHAPTER 140 ୭

YOUR HEARTS REMAIN HARD WITHOUT RESPONSE

JANUARY 2, 2009

"Dear children! While great heavenly grace is being lavished upon you, your hearts remain hard and without response. My children, why do you not give me your hearts completely? I only desire to put in them peace and salvation - my Son. With my Son your soul will be directed to noble goals and you will never get lost. Even in greatest darkness you will find the way. My children decide for a new life with the name of my Son on your lips. Thank you. "

❧ CHAPTER 141 ❧
YOUR TIME IS A SHORT TIME

JUNE 2, 2006

Our Lady did not give a classical message. She blessed all of us who were present and all the religious articles that we brought with us for blessing. With a serious expression on her face, Our Lady emphasized again the priestly blessing. With pain and love at the same time Our Lady said:

"Remember, children of mine, that it is my Son blessing you. Do not accept it so lightly." After that Our Lady told me about some things that are supposed to happen and she said: "There is no way without my Son. Do not think that you will have peace and joy if you do not have Him in the first place." Mirjana said: "I cannot say that Our Lady was sad or joyful; she was preoccupied, with loving care on her face."

NOVEMBER 2, 2006

"My coming to you, my children, is God's Love. God is sending me to warn you and to show you the right way. Do not shut your eyes before the truth, my children. Your time is a short time. Do not permit delusions to begin ruling over you. The way on, which I desire to lead you, is the way of peace and love. This is the way, which leads to my Son, your God. Give me your hearts that I may put my Son in them and make my apostles of you - apostles of peace and love. Thank you!" Afterwards, in conclusion, Our Lady said for us: "Not to forget our shepherds in our prayers."

❧ CHAPTER 142 ❧
YOUR WOUNDED AND RESTLESS HEARTS

MARCH 2, 2009

"Dear Children! I am here among you. I am looking into your wounded and restless hearts. You have become lost, my children. Your wounds from sin are becoming greater and are distancing you all the more from the real truth. You are seeking hope and consolation in the wrong places, while I am offering to you sincere devotion which is nurtured by love, sacrifice and truth. I am giving you my son."

☙ CHAPTER 143 ❧
2012 MESSAGES

MONTHLY MESSAGES

JANUARY 25, 2012

"Dear children! With joy, also today I call you to open your hearts and to listen to my call. Anew, I desire to draw you closer to my Immaculate Heart, where you will find refuge and peace. Open yourselves to prayer, until it becomes a joy for you. Through prayer, the Most High will give you an abundance of grace and you will become my extended hands in this restless world which longs for peace. Little children, with your lives witness faith and pray that faith may grow day by day in your hearts. I am with you. Thank you for having responded to my call."

FEBRUARY 25, 2012

"Dear children! At this time, in a special way I call you: 'pray with the heart'. Little children, you speak much and pray little. Read and meditate on Sacred Scripture, and may the words written in it be life for you. I encourage and love you, so that in God you may find your peace and the joy of living. Thank you for having responded to my call."

MARCH 25, 2012

"Dear children! Also today, with joy, I desire to give you my motherly blessing and to call you to prayer. May prayer become a need for you to grow more in holiness every day. Work more on your conversion because you are far away, little children. Thank you for having responded to my call."

APRIL 25, 2012

"Dear children! Also today I am calling you to prayer, and may your heart, little children, open towards God as a flower opens towards the warmth of the sun. I am with you and I intercede for all of you. Thank you for having responded to my call."

MAY 25, 2012

"Dear children! Also today I call you to conversion and to holiness. God desires to give you joy and peace through prayer but you, little children, are still far away - attached to the earth and to earthly things. Therefore, I call you anew: open your heart and your sight towards God and the things of God - and joy and peace will come to reign in your hearts. Thank you for having responded to my call."

JUNE 25, 2012

"Dear children! With great hope in the heart, also today I call you to prayer. If you pray, little children, you are with me and you are seeking the will of my Son and are living it. Be open and live prayer and, at every moment, may it be for you the savor and joy of your soul. I am with you and I intercede for all of you before my Son Jesus. Thank you for having responded to my call."

JULY 25, 2012

"Dear children! Today I call you to the 'good'. Be carriers of peace and goodness in this world. Pray that God may give you the strength so that hope and pride may always reign in your heart and life because you are God's children and carriers of His hope to this world that is without joy in the heart, and is without a future, because it does not have its heart open to God who is your salvation. Thank you for having responded to my call."

AUGUST 25, 2012

"Dear children! Also today, with hope in the heart, I am praying for you and am thanking the Most High for every one of you who lives my messages with the heart. Give thanks to God's love that I can love and lead each of you through my Immaculate Heart also toward conversion. Open your hearts and decide for holiness, and hope will give birth to joy in your hearts. Thank you for having responded to my call."

SEPTEMBER 25, 2012

"Dear children! When in nature you look at the richness of the colors which the Most High gives to you, open your heart and pray with gratitude for all the good that you have and say: 'I am here created for eternity' – and yearn for heavenly things because God loves you with immeasurable love. This is why He also gave me to you to tell you: 'Only in God is your peace and hope, dear children'. Thank you for having responded to my call."

OCTOBER 25, 2012

"Dear children! Today I call you to pray for my intentions. Renew fasting and prayer because Satan is cunning and attracts many hearts to sin and perdition. I call you, little children, to holiness and to live in grace. Adore my Son so that He may fill you with His peace and love for which you yearn. Thank you for having responded to my call."

NOVEMBER 25, 2012

"Dear children! In this time of grace, I call all of you to renew prayer. Open yourselves to Holy Confession so that each of you may accept my call with the whole heart. I am with you and I protect you from the ruin of sin, but you must open yourselves to the way of conversion and holiness, that your heart may burn out of love for God. Give Him time and He will give Himself to you and thus, in the will of God you will discover the love and the joy of living. Thank you for having responded to my call."

DECEMBER 25, 2012

"Our Lady came with little Jesus in her arms and she did not give a message, but little Jesus began to speak and said: "I am your peace, live my commandments." With a sign of the cross, Our Lady and little Jesus blessed us together."

JANUARY 25, 2013

"Dear children! Also today I call you to prayer. May your prayer be as strong as a living stone, until with your lives you become witnesses. Witness the beauty of your faith. I am with you and intercede before my Son for each of you. Thank you for having responded to my call."

MESSAGES TO MIRJANA SOLO ON 2ND OF THE MONTH

JANUARY 2, 2012

"Dear children! As with motherly concern I look in your hearts, in them I see pain and suffering; I see a wounded past and an incessant search; I see my children who desire to be happy but do not know how. Open yourselves to the Father. That is the way to happiness, the way by which I desire to lead you. God the Father never leaves His children alone, especially not in pain and despair. When you comprehend and accept this, you will be happy. Your search will end. You will love and you will not be afraid. Your life will be hope and truth which is my Son. Thank you. I implore you, pray for those whom my Son has chosen. Do not judge because you will all be judged."

FEBRUARY 2, 2012

"Dear children! I am with you for so much time and already for so long I have been pointing you to God's presence and His infinite love, which I desire for all of you to come to know. And you, my children? You continue to be deaf and blind as you look at the world around you and do not want to see where it is going without my Son. You are renouncing Him - and He is the source of all graces. You listen to me while I am speaking to you, but your hearts are closed and you are not hearing me. You are not praying to the Holy Spirit to illuminate you. My children, pride has come to rule. I am pointing out humility to you. My children, remember that only a humble soul shines with purity and beauty because it has come to know the love of God. Only a humble soul becomes heaven, because my Son is in it. Thank you. Again I implore you to pray for those whom my Son has chosen - those are your shepherds."

MARCH 2, 2012

"Dear children! Through the immeasurable love of God I am coming among you and I am persistently calling you into the arms of my Son. With a motherly heart I am imploring you, my children, but I am also repeatedly warning you, that concern for those who have not come to know my Son be in the first place for you. Do not permit that by looking at you and your life, they are not overcome by a desire to come to know Him.

Pray to the Holy Spirit for my Son to be impressed within you. Pray that you can be apostles of the divine light in this time of darkness and hopelessness. This is a time of your trial. With a rosary in hand and love in the heart set out with me. I am leading you towards Easter in my Son. Pray for those whom my Son has chosen that they can always live through Him and in Him - the High Priest. Thank you."

APRIL 2, 2012

"Dear Children, as the Queen of Peace, I desire to give peace to you, my children, true peace which comes through the heart of my Divine Son. As a mother I pray that wisdom, humility and goodness may come to reign in your hearts – that peace may reign – that my Son may reign. When my Son will be the ruler in your hearts, you will be able to help others to come to know Him. When heavenly peace comes to rule over you, those who are seeking it in the wrong places, thus causing pain to my motherly heart, will recognize it. My children, great will be my joy when I see that you are accepting my words and that you desire to follow me. Do not be afraid, you are not alone. Give me your hands and I will lead you. Do not forget your shepherds. Pray that in their thoughts they may always be with my Son who called them to witness Him. Thank you."

MAY 2, 2012

"Dear children! With motherly love I implore you to give me your hands, permit me to lead you. I, as a mother, desire to save you from restlessness, despair and eternal exile. My Son, by His death on the Cross, showed how much He loves you; He sacrificed Himself for your sake and the sake of your sins. Do not keep rejecting His sacrifice and do not keep renewing His sufferings with your sins. Do not keep shutting the doors of Heaven to yourselves. My children, do not waste time. Nothing is more important than unity in my Son. I will help you because the Heavenly Father is sending me so that, together, we can show the way of grace and salvation to all those who do not know Him. Do not be hard hearted. Have confidence in me and adore my Son. My children, you cannot be without the shepherds. May they be in your prayers every day. Thank you."

JUNE 2, 2012

"Dear children, I am continuously among you because, with my endless love, I desire to show you the door of Heaven. I desire to tell you how it is opened: through goodness, mercy, love and peace - through my Son. Therefore, my children, do not waste time on vanities. Only knowledge of the love of my Son can save you. Through that salvific love and the Holy Spirit He chose me and I, together with Him, am choosing you to be apostles of His love and will. My children, great is the responsibility upon you. I desire that by your example you help sinners regain their sight, enrich their poor souls and bring them back into my embrace. Therefore, pray, pray, fast and confess regularly. If receiving my Son in the Eucharist is the center of your life then do not be afraid, you can do everything. I am with you. Every day I pray for the shepherds and I expect the same of you. Because, my children, without their guidance and strengthening through their blessing, you cannot do it. Thank you."

JULY 2, 2012

"My children; Again, in a motherly way, I implore you to stop for a moment and to reflect on yourselves and on the transience of this your earthly life. Then reflect on eternity and the eternal beatitude. What do you want? Which way do you want to set out on? The Father's love sends me to be a mediatrix for you, to show you with motherly love the way which leads to the purity of soul; a soul unburdened by sin; a soul that will come to know eternity. I am praying that the light of the love of my Son may illuminate you, so that you may triumph over weaknesses and come out of misery. You are my children and I desire for all of you to be on the way of salvation. Therefore, my children, gather around me that I may have you come to know the love of my Son and thus open the door of eternal beatitude. Pray as I do for your shepherds. Again I caution you: do not judge them, because my Son chose them. Thank you."

AUGUST 2, 2012

"Dear children, I am with you and I am not giving up. I desire to have you come to know my Son. I desire for my children to be with me in eternal life. I desire for you to feel the joy of peace and to have eternal salvation. I am praying that you may overcome human weaknesses. I am imploring my Son to give you pure hearts. My dear children, only pure hearts know how to carry a cross and know how to sacrifice for all those sinners who have offended the Heavenly Father and who, even today, offend Him, although they have not come to know Him. I am praying that you may come to know the light of true faith which comes only from prayer of pure hearts. It is then that all those who are near you will feel the love of my Son. Pray for those whom my Son has chosen to lead you on the way to salvation. May your mouth refrain from every judgment. Thank you."

SEPTEMBER 2, 2012
"Dear children, as my eyes are looking at you, my soul is seeking those souls with whom it desires to be one – the souls who have understood the importance of prayer for those of my children who have not come to know the love of the Heavenly Father. I am calling you because I need you. Accept the mission and do not be afraid, I will strengthen you. I will fill you with my graces. With my love I will protect you from the evil spirit. I will be with you. With my presence I will console you in difficult moments. Thank you for your open hearts. Pray for priests. Pray that the unity between my Son and them may be all the stronger, that they may be one. Thank you."

OCTOBER 2, 2012
"Dear children, I am calling you and am coming among you because I need you. I need apostles with a pure heart. I am praying, and you should also pray, that the Holy Spirit may enable and lead you, that He may illuminate you and fill you with love and humility. Pray that He may fill you with grace and mercy. Only then will you understand me, my children. Only then will you understand my pain because of those who have not come to know the love of God. Then you will be able to help me. You will be my light-bearers of God's love. You will illuminate the way for those who have been given eyes but do not want to see. I desire for all of my children to see my Son. I desire for all of my children to experience His Kingdom. Again I call you and implore you to pray for those whom my Son has called. Thank you."

NOVEMBER 2, 2012

"Dear children, as a mother I implore you to persevere as my apostles. I am praying to my Son to give you Divine wisdom and strength. I am praying that you may discern everything around you according to God's truth and to strongly resist everything that wants to distance you from my Son. I am praying that you may witness the love of the Heavenly Father according to my Son. My children, great grace has been given to you to be witnesses of God's love. Do not take the given responsibility lightly. Do not sadden my motherly heart. As a mother I desire to rely on my children, on my apostles. Through fasting and prayer you are opening the way for me to pray to my Son for Him to be beside you and for His name to be holy through you. Pray for the shepherds because none of this would be possible without them. Thank you."

DECEMBER 2, 2012

"Dear children, with motherly love and motherly patience anew I call you to live according to my Son, to spread His peace and His love, so that, as my apostles, you may accept God's truth with all your heart and pray for the Holy Spirit to guide you. Then you will be able to faithfully serve my Son, and show His love to others with your life. According to the love of my Son and my love, as a mother, I strive to bring all of my strayed children into my motherly embrace and to show them the way of faith. My children, help me in my motherly battle and pray with me that sinners may become aware of their sins and repent sincerely. Pray also for those whom my Son has chosen and consecrated in His name. Thank you."

JANUARY 2, 2013

"Dear children, with much love and patience I strive to make your hearts like unto mine. I strive, by my example, to teach you humility, wisdom and love because I need you; I cannot do without you my children. According to God's will I am choosing you, by His strength I am strengthening you. Therefore, my children, do not be afraid to open your hearts to me. I will give them to my Son and in return, He will give you the gift of Divine peace. You will carry it to all those whom you meet, you will witness God's love with your life and you will give the gift of my

Son through yourselves. Through reconciliation, fasting and prayer, I will lead you. Immeasurable is my love. Do not be afraid. My children, pray for the shepherds. May your lips be shut to every judgment, because do not forget that my Son has chosen them and only He has the right to judge. Thank you."

FEBRUARY 2, 2013

"Dear children, love is bringing me to you - the love which I desire to teach you also - real love; the love which my Son showed you when He died on the Cross out of love for you; the love which is always ready to forgive and to ask for forgiveness. How great is your love? My motherly heart is sorrowful as it searches for love in your hearts. You are not ready to submit your will to God's will out of love. You cannot help me to have those who have not come to know God's love to come to know it, because you do not have real love. Consecrate your hearts to me and I will lead you. I will teach you to forgive, to love your enemies and to live according to my Son. Do not be afraid for yourselves. In afflictions my Son does not forget those who love. I will be beside you. I will implore the Heavenly Father for the light of eternal truth and love to illuminate you. Pray for your shepherds so that through your fasting and prayer they can lead you in love. Thank you."

YEARLY MESSAGE TO MIRJANA SOLO

MARCH 18, 2012

"Dear children! I am coming among you because I desire to be your mother - your intercessor. I desire to be the bond between you and the Heavenly Father - your mediatrix. I desire to take you by the hand and to walk with you in the battle against the impure spirit. My children, consecrate yourselves to me completely. I will take your lives into my motherly hands and I will teach them peace and love, and then I will give them over to my Son. I am asking of you to pray and fast because only in this way will you know how to witness my Son in the right way through my motherly heart. Pray for your shepherds that, united in my Son, they can always joyfully proclaim the Word of God. Thank you."

YEARLY MESSAGE TO IVANKA KVANKOVIC

JUNE 25, 2012

At Her last daily apparition on May 7, 1985, Our Lady confided to Ivanka the 10th secret and told her that she would have an apparition once a year on the anniversary of the apparitions. It was that way also this year.

The apparition, which lasted 7 minutes, took place at Ivanka's family home. Only Ivanka's family was present at the apparition. After the apparition, Ivanka said: Our Lady spoke to me about the 5th secret and at the end said:

"I am giving you my motherly blessing. Pray for peace, peace, peace."

YEARLY MESSAGE TO JAKOV COLO

DECEMBER 25, 2012

At the last daily apparition to Jakov Colo on September 12th, 1998, Our Lady told him that henceforth he would have one apparition a year, every December 25th, on Christmas Day. This is also how it was this year. The apparition began at 2:15 pm and lasted 10 minutes. Afterwards Jakov transmitted this message:

"Dear children, give the gift of your life to me and completely surrender to me so that I may help you to comprehend my motherly love and the love of my Son for you. My children, I love you immeasurably and today, in a special way, on the day of the birth of my Son, I desire to receive each of you into my heart and to give a gift of your lives to my Son. My children, Jesus loves you and gives you the grace to live in His mercy, but sin has overtaken many of your hearts and you live in darkness. Therefore, my children, do not wait, say 'no' to sin and surrender your hearts to my Son, because only in this way will you be able to live God's mercy and, with Jesus in your hearts, set out on the way of salvation."

AUTHORS' COMMENTS

We have been following the appearances of Our Lady in Medjugorje for over 20 years, and have read her messages many times, and still do so daily. As a result of producing "Dear Children," we have become very familiar with what she is asking us to do. However, knowing what she is asking and making it a part of our life can be difficult for us to do. Some followers of Medjugorje over the years have lost interest, as they waited for events to unfold. We all want God to intervene in our world and convert all of mankind, but mankind is not cooperating. We want to see things happen now, but God in His mercy gives us more time at the request of His Holy Mother.

Although Mary has been appearing for almost 32 years, she hasn't given up on us. We need to be patient with her. We also need to thank God for this extended period of His mercy. Each time she gives a message, she graciously says, *"Thank you for having responded to my call."*

For those that have lost interest and are not listening, Our Lady needs you to respond to her call again.

For those of us who have been listening, we need to make a greater response for Our Lady.

This is the final battle for the salvation of our families, friends, co-workers, parishioners and all of mankind. Our Lady has said she needs us. We are her soldiers and we are on the front line trying to help Mary win as many souls as we can for God. In a few of her messages she said, *"Courage Children"* and again *"Follow me."* Our Lady is leading us in this battle and she is out in the front. Let's follow her by living her messages. Because of our human nature, this is not always easy. One Lent, she said, *"Turn off your television."* That   is the best place to start. We need to practice moderation and learn to focus our priorities on what is important and beneficial. She realizes how difficult this is for all of us, so she has promised to help us. In the recent message, she said,

Dear children! In this special time of your effort to be all the closer to my Son, to His suffering, but also to the love with which He bore it, I desire to tell you that I am with you. **I will help you to triumph over errors and temptations** *with my grace. I will teach you love, love which wipes away all sins and makes you perfect, love which gives you the peace of my Son now and forever. Peace with you and in you, because I am the Queen of Peace. Thank you.*

She will help us with God's grace to overcome sin and to become perfect. She will teach us love. To be successful in living her heavenly messages, all we need to do is ask her for help. Jesus has entrusted His grace to her to give to us if we ask her for help. Our prayer is as simple as the song in the Miraculous Medal devotion: *"Mother dearest, Mother fairest, help us, help us we pray."*

May Our Lady of Medjugorje bless all of you with her Motherly blessing and give you God's grace and peace.

Order these books from Two Hearts Press
at www.TwoHeartsPress.com or call 800-BookLog (266-5564)